Rapid Knowledge Acquisition & Synthesis:

How to Quickly Learn, Comprehend, Apply, and Master New Information and Skills

By Peter Hollins,
Author and Researcher at
petehollins.com

Table of Contents

Table of Contents

Chapter One. Your Obstacles Are Everyone's Obstacles
　It's not about smarts
　Maybe it's all about avoiding failure
　More effective goal formation
　Style, format, and sources

Chapter Two. The Double Loop Framework
　Single and double loop learning
　The theory-in-use
　Adapt and grow

Chapter Three. Reading 2.0
　Four steps to reading
　SQ3R

Chapter Four. Just Ask
　Questions for thought
　Socrates the great

Chapter Five. Notes as Your Second Brain
　The Luhmann method

The Ahrens' method

Chapter Six. Lessons from the Science of Learning
   Technique 1: Self-explanation and purposeful elaboration
   Technique 2: Variety is the spice of information absorption
   Technique 3: What you do when you're not learning
   Technique 4: Perfect practice makes perfect
   Technique 5: Use dual coding

Summary Guide

Chapter One. Your Obstacles Are Everyone's Obstacles

Whether you're a university student, trying to grasp a new skill or simply attempting to improve your performance at work, *learning how to learn* may well be the best skill you ever acquire. Whatever our chosen area of expertise, we'll always fare better if we pay conscious attention to how we learn—whether that's taking more effective notes, processing new information better, quickly comprehending material or simply learning to read lightning fast.

How we learn is what gets us from Point A to Point B; it is the vehicle that we drive, and we can choose to arrive in a rusted jalopy, or a smooth and sleek Ferrari.

We often assume there is only one way to learn, or that people will naturally find the optimal approach without trying too hard. We believe everyone learns through processes that they are most comfortable, and thus productive, with. Nothing could be further from the truth—effective learning is a "meta skill" that improves our ability to learn all other skills, and it's something we need to deliberately and consistently cultivate in ourselves if we hope to improve.

This book is about learning—about how to become better at acquiring, processing and retaining knowledge and skills of all kinds. Learning is a complex process of being aware of, managing, comprehending, absorbing, synthesizing and recalling information on an ongoing basis. The better we're able to manipulate and handle information according to our goals and needs, the more deeply we understand, and the more thorough our learning process.

With that being said, why do so few people spend time developing their ability to learn? Why is there not more attention paid to learning for its own sake, or to sharpening those abilities that support and enable all our other ones?

Unfortunately, becoming better at learning is seldom easy. There are obstacles that prevent people from fully exploring their intellectual potential, and have them operating at a lower, less efficient level out of pure habit. This is why we'll begin this book not with the techniques themselves, but with all the things that ordinarily impede our mastery of them. In removing our own resistance, we gain better access to better learning.

It's not about smarts

Can you think of any potential obstacles to learning? If you're like most people, you might have listed poor time management, not having great study skills or simply lacking intelligence.

Maybe the kind of environments where you typically try to learn—home, school, etc.—

haven't been the most conducive to acquiring knowledge. Distractions, and negative past experiences such as bad teachers or boring, one-dimensional school curricula, are all reasons why someone might be turned off by the concept of learning something new. In rare cases, obstacles might also be presented by physical disabilities such as perceptual or memory issues.

The truth, however, is that most learning attempts are jeopardized way before you get to the stage of sitting down to learn. In other words, the obstacles that are most likely to derail your effective learning are usually *psychological* and *behavioral*, not strategic. This means that improving your methods may have a very limited effect in the first instance if you haven't addressed the deeper barriers that are preventing you from ever getting started with them.

Firstly, this is not a matter of laziness or a poor attitude. In fact, many of the mental and psychological obstacles we'll discuss here are simply part of human nature, or are otherwise encouraged and even rewarded in our workplaces, schools and society in general.

Human beings want to learn, in many cases, because they desire *mastery*. What is mastery except the ability to control and command something? Instead of being at the mercy of an unknown, we might seek to dismantle and understand it, so that it's *us* who can then manipulate, control or predict the phenomena we confront in the world around us.

But it's this need for control that can actually backfire in the learning process. In our struggle to retain control, and to avoid any state of vulnerability or ignorance, we may act in ways that actually limit our perspective and keep us failing harder and for longer.

Stemming from this larger unconscious motivation is the need to think of learning as mere problem-solving, as something we do to "win"—over our colleagues, over our own weakness, over nature itself. It follows then that we'll be squeamish and intolerant of "losing" (or what we characterize as losing) and so behave, again, in ways that actually ensure we lose all the more often. This is often a question of ego, pride, and the avoidance of the nasty feeling of failure. As you may have noticed in other areas of your life, this avoidance of pain can be a quite powerful motivator.

Using learning and knowledge acquisition as a means to increase control also encourages us to be as "rational" as possible, to be infallible, perfect, complete. We will want things to follow neat, orderly and linear logic and be unable to bear uncertainty or ambiguity with any patience or nuance. Again, by doing so we only close down our field of possibility and force a narrower vision of learning on ourselves.

An attitude that approaches learning in this way may work in some contexts, for some of the time, but it will never be as good as approaching learning with a truly open, curious mind—one that is receptive, creative and willing to tolerate the unknown or feelings of incompetence along the road to mastery. One attitude is expansive, open-ended and curious. The other is fearful, controlling and narrowing. Both can lead to learning, but one path will be far easier and more successful!

Being "bad at learning" is seldom a question of technique and more a problem of attitude or perspective. Today, there is a popular model proposed by psychology professor Carol Dweck outlining the difference between a "growth mindset" and a "fixed mindset." This model closely mirrors the fundamental differences in attitude one might bring to learning.

A fixed mindset is just that—fixed. Static. This is the person who insists that the experience of life come to them in a predictable, unalterable way. This is the person who believes that human abilities are inborn and that you either have or don't have. Creativity, intelligence or being a fast learner are simply attributes you possess in an unchanging way.

A fixed mindset implies a view of the world and yourself that downplays deep and genuine learning. After all, if you are already all that you can be; what more *is* there to learn? It would be largely impossible, beyond a few tiny improvements. You look at other successful people and assume that things were simply easier for them because they were smarter or more talented.

This close identification between skill and identity also means that failure is not just failure—it's a damning statement about your worth as a human being. You don't fail, you *are* a failure. With a fixed mindset, not understanding or knowing something is embarrassing and experienced as a deficit in character—something that should be hidden or denied. Not exactly the right conditions for learning to occur!

On the other hand, a growth mindset sees learning in an entirely different light, as something that is dynamic, constantly moving, and always possible to change. With this mindset, we don't see ourselves as saddled with an unchanging set of abilities, but rather as living and developing beings who can grow and improve with effort.

Whereas a person with a fixed mindset will give up quickly (why try when you can't do it immediately and easily?), the person with a growth mindset knows that struggling is just part of the process—they *expect* to feel a little stupid when they begin, and it doesn't stop them.

Failure doesn't threaten their identity. They're OK with making mistakes because it doesn't say anything about who they are. It's merely a step in their journey, and they see all learning as a process that necessarily involves a little trial and error. While the person with a fixed mindset will avoid challenge and gravitate to only those areas where they can be assured of winning, a person with a growth mindset isn't scared off by difficult tasks, by the feeling of being a beginner, or by having to try over and over before getting better.

Put another way, these two mindsets see learning differently—fixed as a means of control, growth as a means of satisfying curiosity. One seeks to dominate and command the skill in question, while the other is willing to approach it humbly, to submit to the learning curve involved and become a disciple (i.e. one who takes a path of conscious discipline) to the *process* of learning, rather than merely wanting to rush to the flashy end result or outcome.

Ironically, it's those people who possess more raw intelligence who may be especially bad at learning. Being blessed with large amounts of talent can easily blind us into thinking that inborn skill is the only thing that matters.

Experts and professionals of all kinds can fall into a trap precisely because they have been primed by their own experience and past expectation—i.e., they are even less able to see the world clearly, with a "beginner's mind" and an open-ended curiosity instead of a blanket assumption about how every problem should be solved.

We also lose the chance to develop learning skills and techniques if we've skated by largely by the luck of a gigantic memory or talent of rapid understanding.

Or, sometimes, we think that we're good at learning when in fact we're only habituated in one small, particular style of thinking that we have learnt over time. We may *think* we are being creative problem solvers, when we are really operating in a very narrow set of assumptions. Similarly, we may believe we are trying to understand the information in front of us, when in fact, what we are doing is not saying "what are you?" but "how can I control you and get the better of you for my own benefit?"

Maybe it's all about avoiding failure

The fixed mindset rears its head in all matters of fear and failure. The inner monologue seems to go like this: "If I fail it will mean that I'm a bad person, and I can't bear that. It's better that I don't even try at all than try and fail." This only has the effect of sabotaging any positive effort and dooming it to failure before we even begin to learn.

This particular obstacle can partner up with the previous one—when we feel pressured into a challenge we don't feel equal to, we can unconsciously avoid, delay or pull back from our learning in an effort to never be judged a failure. If others' expectations of us are high or unreasonable, procrastination can be something of a self-preservation tactic, designed to spare us from not performing up to scratch.

But what's so bad about failure, really?

If we can uncouple our sense of self-worth from our performance, failure will no longer threaten us. Failure isn't something we are, it's merely something we do. A low tolerance for failure (or for poor performance, or bumbling around unskillfully) gives us a clue that we may be operating from a fixed mindset. Author Stephen McCranie said, "A master has failed more times than the beginner has even tried"—and it's true.

Many of the most successful people today have suffered miserable failures before they experienced success. The founder of e-commerce giant Alibaba, Jack Ma, is worth $36 billion today. However, as a college graduate, he was rejected for over thirty jobs, including one at KFC. Speaking of KFC, Colonel Sanders himself was rejected 109 times before someone would believe in his chicken recipe.

Other big names like Walt Disney and Howard Schultz, the founder of Starbucks, similarly faced hundreds of rejections. Yet, their persistence ensured that they would eventually be successful.

The fact is that failure is not only possible, it's likely. It's necessary. The massive proliferation of success stories deludes us into thinking that failure is only for the incompetent, that the successful are fated to be so. But in truth it is our failures that teach us what we need to turn the tide.

When you were a baby, you didn't simply get up one day and start walking perfectly. Instead, you bumbled along over a period of time, sometimes falling over, sometimes needing a little help, sometimes trying a new technique or reverting back to crawling. You would not have learnt to walk any faster if you had been judgmental of yourself, or condemned any fall as a "failure."

When you resist failure, you are in fact resisting learning itself, since the two are inseparable. As Albert Einstein once said, "A person who never made a mistake never tried anything new". A person who is learning a new dance choreography may try to do a complicated move forty times before mastering it. However, if they shy away from those forty "wrong" attempts, they *never* get it right.

If you have a fear of failure, there are a few ways to tackle it:

- Get to the root of what failure (and success) actually means to you

- Work at redefining this definition for yourself, so that you truly accept failure as a necessary and valuable part of the learning process
- Deliberately set out to fail. Make a plan to play around without any goal of how your efforts should look. Try things out, mess around and try to see what doesn't work—the idea is not to perform and be perfect, but to grow, learn and experiment
- Constantly remind yourself that you have value whether you succeed or fail, that who you are has nothing to do with your achievement on any one task
- Try giving yourself mini rewards and accolades along the way, to mark your successes as "checkpoints" on the road to mastery. This will remind you that you *are* learning, even when you feel like you're not making progress

On the other hand, some people may unconsciously fear *success*. Why? It comes down to pressure again. "If I perform well on this, then I set a new precedent and everyone will expect even more from me, and I don't want that." Again the antidote is to disentangle your identity from your performance, and relinquish your focus on the outcome in favor of optimizing the process it takes to get there.

Closely connected to the obstacle of fear of failure is low self-esteem, or the idea that we are worthless, useless or somehow not as good as everyone else. For those suffering from both, failure isn't just a sign of incompetence, it is confirmation of what they suspected all along. If you sincerely believe that you will fail, or even that you are not deserving of success, then you will never really try wholeheartedly, and even if you do succeed at something, you will not acknowledge or enjoy it.

As an example, a student may consistently do poorly at exams not because they are unintelligent or incapable of hard work, but because they don't really believe they are the kind of person who deserves good things in life, or they think success and achievement are really for other people, and not them. Without even knowing it, they may jeopardize themselves, undermining their attempts even before they start, downplaying their achievements and setting up self-fulfilling prophesies that confirm their beliefs about themselves.

To fix the problem, the instinct may be to praise yourself for what you achieve. Teachers often resort to over-the-top compliments and admiration to get a student to believe in themselves, but this can backfire. As long as a person believes their value as a human being is tied into their performance on a task, they will never possess true self-esteem (or any sense of their own inner drive and motivation). An authentically confident person is able to say, "I did poorly on this task. That's OK. I'm going to try harder next time" and never once assumes that they are lazy, bad, stupid or untalented.

On the other hand, a confident person will also approach their achievements in the same way: "I did well on this task. That's great, but I'm going to keep going," without ever thinking that they are finished with learning for good and can now rest on their laurels. Again, it's the difference between a growth and fixed mindset.

Sometimes, focusing on the final goal can be debilitating, since it only reinforces how far you have to go. Instead, if low self-esteem is tripping up your learning, try as much as possible to forget about the end goal, at least for a while. Make smaller targets or create objectives that are related to your effort and not the outcome.

For example, tell yourself that you will spend an hour on your new venture each day, or read a chapter, or work on one section of your project. These goals are always achievable, whether you succeed or not. Goals like "get an A," "beat my previous time" or "win such and such award" are trickier because you are not always in control of whether these will be fulfilled or not. You are *always* in control, however, of how much effort you make and the attitude you have when you pitch up to learn.

More effective goal formation

Having said that, goals are still important. However, it's worth thinking about different kinds of goals, and the different functions they could serve. You've probably heard that it's wise to make SMART goals—i.e. those that are Specific, Measurable, Attainable, Relevant and Time-Sensitive. This means that it's better to say, "To improve my conversational English, I'm going to learn fifty new English phrasal verbs by the end of the month" instead of "I'm going to get better at English."

Goals, however, can go further than this. We've seen that it's easier to achieve process goals ("I'm going to study ten hours") versus outcome goals ("I'm going to pass with a distinction"), but a goal is more than just a marker you set in the future. It's a commitment, and a conscious decision for an intention that's important to you.

Your objective can be anything you want it to be; you could, for example, simply set the goal that you will face all the challenges you encounter in a new learning module with patience and determination. This is a goal about the meta-learning process itself, rather than the specific content you're studying.

Goals always work best when they tap into your deeper motivation. We've seen that its harder to work on a thing that you don't genuinely care about. Goals need to speak to your inner desires, and the reason *why* you are learning in the first place. It can be useful to imagine how you will be different once you have learnt what you need to learn or acquired the skills you want to acquire.

Becoming better at anything is so much more than just acquiring certain skills or bits of knowledge—it also comes with a shift in perspective and attitude. Perhaps a more global, creative or compassionate worldview. Perhaps the maturity to not be freaked out by mistakes. Perhaps the experience gained from having to be patient and trusting as the learning unfolds. The ability to take responsibility, to be proactive, to dig into what the goal really *means* for you….

If you can understand the motivational engine behind your goals, you know how to tap into that when learning is difficult. Whether you're simply trying to learn something small and quick, or attempting a grand project that will take many years, your aim is essentially to transform who you are now into the version of yourself that is proficient in this area.

What will that look like? And what will that take? Find out what your motivation is and you have won half the battle!

Style, format, and sources

Some barriers to your learning are obvious—the information you need to take onboard is simply presented in a confusing way that hinders your understanding, rather than helps it. If you've ever had a terrible lecturer at university, you'll know what a big difference presentation can make!

Unhelpful learning environments can undo all your hard work. Think about the effect of constant interruptions, distractions, an environment that is too hot or cold, noisy, not bright enough, not private, or not comfortable.

Think also about the form your learning materials take—are you relying heavily on text-based materials when you're a more practically oriented, hands-on learner? Are you using poor quality or outdated tools or practicing with exercises or instruments that are too advanced for you?

Especially if you're embarking on self-teaching, you need to pay special attention to supporting your learning in every way possible. Invest time and energy into getting the right materials, tools, software, ingredients, teachers, and so on that you'll need to do your best.

Often, you'll find that discovering these support materials only takes minimal effort. Depending on the type of resources and the specific topic you're trying to learn about, a few Google searches might well suffice in pointing you to productive tools for learning. However, keep in mind that popularity does not necessarily mean utility, and learning is not one size fits all. The fact that many people have tried or even found a particular resource helpful does not mean you will too. Instead, focus on descriptions and make informed choices based on them.

If one mode of learning isn't working for you, you don't need to force yourself along—try something different. Ask a different teacher, source study guides or online forums, watch YouTube videos or get a practiced expert to show you in person. Listen to audiobooks or take notes according to your own learning preference. The more you mix things up, the better (we'll explore this more later in the book).

If you're not doing well with some study materials, you might find you can learn a lot by designing your own improved materials, or supplementing as you see fit. Whatever your area of learning, use plenty of imagery and metaphor, mnemonics, video and audio, presentations or podcasts, webinars, tutorials, hands-on practice, mind mapping diagrams, summarizing or even compiling a lesson to teach others. The important thing is that you proactively take charge of your own learning. If you encounter difficulties, become curious about *why*, and find a path around it.

If you're disorganized, spend an afternoon devising your own protocols that are completely unique to you. If you're unimpressed with your teacher or trainer, get another one, or seek out a few different teaching perspectives.

Sometimes, you learn best when you are forced to forge your own path. Be glad when you have the opportunity to really puzzle your way through a challenge—it's often the knowledge you attain while struggling that is best anchored in your mind.

Takeaways

- Learning new things to increase your knowledge and skill set sounds good in theory, but many of us hesitate to try learning something new. We cite common excuses like not having enough time, not having access to good resources, or fearing failure in new endeavors. Our years in school have left us with the impression that learning is one-dimensional and utterly boring. Yet this is far from the case. Here is where learning *how* to learn becomes so important.
- Those of us who are afraid to learn are often unknowingly suffering from a fixed mindset. This way of thinking assumes that people are born with a static set of qualities and talents that never change. If we aren't immediately successful at something, we just don't have what it takes. Yet this sort of thinking is extraordinarily unhelpful, as it prevents us from exposing ourselves to new skills and knowledge. Fixed mindsets are particularly common in people who

fear failure, have low self-esteem, or excuse themselves by pretending to be too busy. For them, failure isn't a natural part of learning, but a damning indictment of one's abilities. They fail to recognize that mistakes are as natural as breathing, and that learning well necessarily involves failing, and failing repeatedly.
- However, if we adopt a growth mindset wherein the possibilities for development and expansion are endless, we find that we are much more open to learning, as well as failure in learning. Some common issues that people face when trying to learn new things include not forming their goals properly, and failing to discover good resources to study. While both of these issues are surmountable for those with a growth mindset, they become impossible to overcome if you have a fixed mindset that refuses to consider more than one option. As such, cultivating a growth mindset is

essential to learning new skills and acquiring more knowledge.

Chapter Two. The Double Loop Framework

The double loop model of learning is not so much a fixed technique as a shift in perspective or mindset. It's a new approach to taking in, synthesizing and retaining the information we want to learn, whether that's a new motor skill, a language, or academic material for an important exam. And it's one that is necessary for the goals of this book.

To make it work, we need to be willing to abandon the old, conventional learning models that we all learned in school. Though we may gravitate toward these out of habit, we need to constantly remind ourselves that the knee-jerk way of doing things is not necessarily the most effective or efficient. The way we've done things, the assumptions we've held, and everything up until this point could be wrong.

The double loop learning framework makes you embraces this for better knowledge acquisition and comprehension. There's a reason that many athletic trainers would prefer to train someone starting from scratch rather than someone with a little bit of prior experience; that prior experience or knowledge can lead to skewed beliefs or habits.

Again, we need to get back to basics and change our definition of learning. Typically, we think of learning like a predictable ladder—one step at a time. School coursework is designed like this: you finish one level and then move onto the next, block by block. A, B, C, D, and so on in a forward, linear fashion.

But there's an alternative to this linear model—a circular one in which A leads to B, B leads to C, but then C can also lead back into A again. In a linear model, you can only advance or fall down (reminds you of the fixed mindset and its conception of failure, doesn't it?) but in a loop you are always in process, always learning (i.e. working within a growth mindset and having "beginner's mind").

In linear models, learning establishes a hierarchy—twelfth graders know more than tenth graders, and bosses know better than their employees. In a loop model, people only compete against themselves, and everyone is merely at a particular point in their process, which is neither better nor worse than any other point.

In a learning loop, you can always improve, and in fact you can sustain yourself forever, continually developing skills and knowledge using constant feedback and starting at the "beginning" again. From this point of view, there is never really any finish line or big prize at the end. Learning is more like an ongoing way of life, it just requires you to honestly assess yourself from time to time.

Consider a researcher who finds some interesting correlations between two diseases that were previously assumed to be unconnected. One stage of her learning is to conduct experiments on participants she's gathered. She publishes her findings and her work is read by another professional from an entirely new field—and he has some interesting findings of his own to share. The researcher takes this new data and devises another experiment to test fresh hypotheses, learning more and more from other colleagues weighing in on her original publication…

Here, there is no end goal, no point at which the researcher can say she's finished, or has reached the top of the pile. Instead, her learning inspires yet more learning, her questions spur further questions, and she is taking part in a growing and evolving process rather than a simplistic journey from A to B.

Single and double loop learning

Simply being in a loop is not necessarily all that useful, however. After all, you could be repeating the same error over and over again, or engaging in a feedback loop that only compounds and amplifies any mistakes you made the first time around. Understanding this allows us to see the difference between single and double loops.

Consider this (simplified) learning loop:

Step 1: Lift heavy weights at the gym.
Step 2: When a weight becomes too easy to lift, move up to a heavier weight. Return to Step 1.

Following this protocol, you will most likely end up gaining muscle strength and becoming more fit at the gym. At the very least, you'll ensure that you're always lifting the heaviest weight you possibly can. But compare it to the following:

Step 1: Lift heavy weights at the gym.
Step 2: When a weight becomes too easy to lift, move up to a heavier weight.

Step 3: Track your progress and ask why you're advancing—or not.

Step 4: Identify possible impediment to advancing with heavier weights—consider time of day when training, diet, supplements taken, hydration, mood and recovery time.

Step 5: Isolate each factor and run experiments—i.e. does having fewer rest days actually make training more difficult?

Step 6: Adjust schedule according to findings from Step 5.

Step 7: Return to step 3 and repeat.

The above contains more than one loop, and these feed back dynamically into one another. This is better learning in a nutshell. It is harder, more involved, and leads to undoubtedly better outcomes.

Professor Chris Argyris at Harvard Business School explains that double loop learning, as you can see, is more complex.

In this learning mode, you are constantly zooming in and out of the process, adjusting, factoring in and re-appraising, shifting mental models depending on what works, and so on. Argyris believes that we all have mental maps or cognitive schemas that we work from whenever we learn something, but we can become more or less conscious about which ones we use and how.

To put it simply, a single loop has you take an action, see the results, and feed back that action into the first step. When you engage in double loop thinking, however, you spend extra time considering the mental models and frameworks you are operating within, looking carefully at how they inspire your actions, and in turn the results you're getting.

Any time you learn to learn, or investigate the way you ask questions, or evaluate the outcomes of your evaluation technique, then you are adding that extra layer of complexity that gives more insight into what is actually happening on a deeper level.

Single loop learning is fine if you're a machine, but it has its weaknesses. It's a fixed process. If there's a problem, there's no real way to *see* that there's a problem, or respond to it. The only choices are to stop or carry on.

In some cases, we can respond to problems that crop up in single loop learning mechanisms. We take an action, find that the result doesn't match our expected outcome, make some changes to the action, and hope for a better result. However, with this method of rectifying errors we only end up working on symptoms, while the root cause of those mistakes is left unnoticed.

Following this model tempts us into believing that if only we modified our own actions a little, our results would be better. In reality, the number of factors affecting successful learning are far greater than what single loop learning allows for.

With double loop learning, however, you have the opportunity to question underlying assumptions, and the chance to fix and improve them for better outcomes. You are no longer blindly acting, but consciously designing the most optimal way of proceeding. To connect this idea to those we explored in the previous chapter, you might notice that a fixed mindset or a need for control encourages single loop learning, whereas a growth mindset or one founded on genuine curiosity is more likely to lead to double loop learning.

It's simple: fear of failure, craving control and certainty, ego, not wanting to appear wrong or stupid, intolerance for the unknown or for being in process… all of these establish a mental model that, when unexamined, puts you on a single loop path that won't necessarily lead to improvement.

Double loop learning is harder. It requires time, patience, and humility to dismantle mental models that aren't working for you. Most people would prefer to stay firmly *inside* their mental model and assume that it's all there is, and solve their problems from within this deliberately limited perspective.

Some of the hardest work in this area is acknowledging that you are in fact inhabiting a mental model at all. The most difficult perspectives to shift are those that you simply experience as reality itself, as natural, inviolable laws that you have never stopped to consider alternatives to, or even the *possibility* of alternatives.

Whenever we face a problem or some novel situation in life, we can deal with it based on our previous experience. However, the very essence of learning something new is doing and discovering what you didn't do or know before! If you approach new information or situations using only the same old rules you've learned from the past, you risk oversimplifying things, or missing enormous aspects of what's in front of you.

Addressing the problem from our static inventory of mental tools is a necessary *first* step, but if we hope to make qualitative leaps in these skills themselves, we can't help but focus on our learning methods, and ask how and whether they're working.

The theory-in-use

You may be entirely unconscious of the inner theory you have about the world—i.e., what Argyris called an "espoused theory of action." He, along with his fellow researchers, found that our espoused theory of certain actions is often different from our "theory-in-use," which is the theory based on which we actually act.

Let's consider an example from Argyris's research. A management consultant is asked how he would deal with a disagreement involving a certain client. The consultant responds that he would start by stating the way he understood the disagreement, and then negotiate how they could come to an agreement based on relevant data. However, a tape of the consultant when faced with such a predicament revealed that he simply dismissed his client's opinion and advocated for his own views. The former was his espoused theory, while the later was his theory-in-use.

Any decision, reaction or challenge that we face can be passed through this theory and interpreted accordingly with single loop learning.

The trouble is when you don't allow yourself to solve a problem or learn something new any *other* way. "Thinking out of the box" is something that sounds great, but is actually seldom done. When we feel powerless to change the way something works, like if we have a fixed mindset, it can feel comfortable to simply assume that things are the way they are and that nothing you do will impact that arrangement in any significant way. According to that view, our problems aren't necessarily the result of our own actions, but merely a consequence of the way things are.

When was the last time you questioned the underlying "rules" of the game you're playing, be it at school, in the workplace or in your chosen arena of expertise? When did you last take a genuinely holistic view of the choices you made and accepted responsibility for them? When did you accurately detect an error in the way you were seeing things, and have the courage to adapt?

This last question is perhaps the most pertinent. A perfectionist or someone dominated by fear, control, or ego will look at a pristine track record and see the absence of "errors" as a good sign. Isn't it great to be *right*? However, the opposite is likely true.

Deep learning happens when a person is capable of accurately detecting errors, inefficiencies or weaknesses in their own process, *and* is capable of making the relevant changes. When you think about it, how else could learning possibly be? In the same way as you cannot imagine a person all of a sudden speaking fluently in a brand-new language, you cannot picture a learning process that lacks mistakes, and the detection of those mistakes.

We should be striving not to avoid mistakes, but to continually make higher level ones. As the author Jules Verne once said, "Science is made up of mistakes, but they are mistakes which it is useful to make because little by little they lead us to the truth." The same applies to our lives as well. We may be disappointed by errors, but ultimately those errors facilitate improvement if they are properly addressed and rectified.

Again, double loop learning does not entail adjustment at a merely superficial level, i.e. how to run your current single loop more quickly. Rather, it's about taking a step back to look at the loops themselves. Instead of blindly and uncritically following our normal protocol, we take charge and responsibility for managing our own protocols for ourselves. Ironically, it's this attitude that offers the prospect of real control!

Let's look at an example. A history teacher is struggling to engage his class on a chapter about the Industrial Revolution. He has his teacher's toolkit ("The way things are done") and tries it all: disciplining students who chat during class, issuing punishments for those who don't submit homework, yelling, lecturing, and so on.

None of these methods work, and his students still aren't interested in the subject. After a while, the teacher realizes he's been engaging in single loop thinking, merely doubling down on his efforts using the same old tactics over and over.

He takes a broader view. His first question—*why* are the students so uninterested in this topic? He chats to some other teachers who all weigh in and give their advice, and reads up a little about student motivation.

And then it hits him—he's *still* working within the old educational framework that governs how teachers and students relate, and how classroom problems are solved. He understands what he needs to do next: talk to the students.

He realizes, with some surprise, that the students themselves are reflecting back the same problem he's dealing with: they are bored in class because the curriculum is forcing a kind of uninspired single loop learning.

By reflecting on his own process in the classroom, the teacher simultaneously understands what's missing in the material for the students, as well—critical thinking and reflection (i.e. double loop learning). He sees that when single loops are running, people don't really *learn*—they just go round and round.

He changes his approach entirely. The class has a long and lively debate about not only the topic, but about the learning experience itself. He decides to work with the students to look back at all the ways the previous study plan failed. The students step in and engage, feeling inspired and encouraged to design their own curriculum to adapt to changes and new developments.

Far from what it appeared at first, the students are actually intensely interested in the topic and enjoy learning about it and engaging with one another. The teacher finds himself encountering completely new and fresh perspectives that he hadn't considered before. In this case, the single loop itself was preventing deeper and more insightful learning, and the students responded well when fear, hierarchies and stale old assumptions were questioned and updated.

This simple example makes it all seem pretty easy, but of course the quality of your double loop thinking will depend very much on the mental models you're able to use, your decision-making process, your values, your willingness to change and a lot more. It sounds simple enough to modify your learning based on new evidence and experimentation, but this is seldom a very clear-cut process. When you zoom out far enough, almost everything that resembles a learning process, every idea, action, decision, thought, and even feeling can be seen as a part of a particular mental model or perspective.

Whatever it is that you're trying to learn (including the skill of being better at learning), you'll need some kind of framework to help you assess frameworks. You'll need a way to build loops that are dynamic and can grow. You'll need to have ways to identify and remove mistakes, so you don't end up making them again and again.

This is not a merely objective phenomenon—you'll have to be quite honest and discerning enough to weigh up your process and outcomes against your own deeper values. Reflection is a rich and insightful process; it's not merely scanning your code for bugs.

Adapt and grow

Argyris's research suggests that one way in which we can do this is by considering different strategies to attain the outcome that we desire. To go back to the management consultant example, regardless of which theory is at work when he contends with clients, the desired outcome is resolution of conflict. However, instead of going with the theory he espoused or the theory he actually used, he might opt for a third strategy. This could be simply listening to his client's issues instead of outlining his understanding of the dispute.

However, this would be an example of single loop learning. The consultant would only have fixed the symptom—failing to properly resolve conflict with a client—without looking at why he wants to arrive at a peaceful resolution in the first place. If he were to critically examine his motivations to achieve his desired outcome, he might just shift from simply ameliorating a disagreement to creating a meaningful dialogue that leads to mutual benefit. This is what would constitute true double loop learning.

Experience is always useful. But be careful—twenty years' experience might merely be the same single year's experience repeated twenty times over. This is why many experts can actually perform worse in some areas than newbies—they simply face problems in the same way as they have faced all previous problems. What's more, experts may be acting from more fear of failure, need for control or ego than people with less knowledge, since their identities are more bound up in their expertise, and they may feel more threatened by error or the shame of saying "I don't know."

Intelligent and educated people can thus put themselves at a disadvantage, especially if they are not actively seeking ways to adapt and change their mental models (not just the content of those models). The world is constantly changing, and those who stay still are actually falling behind.

Being heavily invested in appearing right, in having mastery, and so on, we make more mistakes and are less likely to notice them and fix them. We may also shy away completely from challenges that could help us grow, or from novel experiences when they fall outside our expectations. We may get trapped in a cycle of simply solving the problem that's directly in front of us, again and again, never having the time or energy to wonder if there's a better way to do it.

We try to avoid pain, discomfort, embarrassment or uncertainty. So, we carry on doing what we know works, even though in the longer term, this may lead to objectively more disadvantages! Ours is a productivity obsessed culture that wants profit and advancement at all costs, constantly, and at breakneck speed. We seldom encourage ourselves or one another to stop and reflect, to appraise, to think more deeply or broadly, to take a more creative route through a problem, or to question authority and convention. But all the more reason to do so!

Time is a complicating factor when it comes to single versus double loop thinking. Many people believe that they don't have time to dwell on hypothetical, blue-sky thinking when they're facing urgent real-world problems . It's hard to commit to something that may or may not work, and will only pay off sometime in the future. Isn't it easier to just carry on as we always did, getting the same predictable but comforting result?

The fact that so many people choose the latter is proof of how difficult the former is. We spend our formative years in schools that teach us methods of thinking that never go beyond single loops (blame the designers of the curriculum for failing to adapt and reflect!). We may have bosses that want us to work in limited roles that consist of a handful of single loops done indefinitely, with no scope for engaging with or adjusting them.

The biggest culprit in cementing single loop thinking is actually success itself. If you are used to succeeding, switching to double loop thinking (where failure and mistakes are essential) may make you may feel defensive and resistant. Smart people may paradoxically be worse learners, because they so seldom make mistakes, and therefore seldom learn from them. When they do slip up, they may deny it, avoid it, or blame someone else. Their intellect makes them unable to step up and learn when it really counts.

Imagine an office run by such an expert. This is the typical boss from hell: they know everything, never admit to mistakes or apologize, and frequently blame underlings for their poor decisions. This is the person who asks for honest opinions during a meeting and then quietly penalizes those who offer them.

Worst of all, this boss assumes that everyone working for him is an idiot, and needs his constant micromanaging. Here we see another hidden effect of fixed, single loop thinking: it sets up self-fulfilling prophecies. The employees, discouraged from critical thinking and never given any chance to make decisions for themselves, end up doing less—why bother when their manager already knows all the answers? Even worse, some employees start to blame one another and seek underhanded tactics to compete for his favor.

The "expert" has created the very conditions he wished to avoid—he now has a team of people who cannot be trusted, and who only want to do the bare minimum to get ahead for their own benefit. A teacher or parent may do the same, or you may do it with yourself, every time you self-jeopardize because of poor self-esteem.

We all hate bad bosses and egotistical leaders, but in the above example, did you identify with the employees or the manager? The truth is, it's hardest of all to look at *ourselves* and ask why a problem is happening, or why we're failing to learn or understand something new.

Simple, defensive loops are a way to avoid effort and pain. But they're also an excellent way of avoiding learning. A foolproof way of noticing whether you're in a single loop pattern is to look for the tendency to blame others and not question the role of your own perspectives and mental models.

It's better to be of mediocre skill and intelligence but a master at learning from mistakes than to be a genius who cannot stand to look at his imperfections at all. Blaming, spinning up complicated justifications or making excuses gets you precisely 0 percent closer to the things you care about.

Invite failure, get experimental, become curious

What paradigm are you working within?
Where did these conventions come from?
Are they working for you?
What habits are you stuck in?
What assumptions are you making?
What unspoken rules are you following?
What is your attitude toward failure?
What's the bigger picture?

Let's return to our history teacher. If he continues refining and adapting his approach as he goes, he may encounter resistance, but he also may start to campaign for real change in not just his school, but classrooms everywhere. He takes what he understands from the chapter on the Industrial Revolution and realizes that schools themselves have modelled their architecture, schedules and curricula on the design principles and ideology that came with that era.

He notices that the working world is desperately trying to move on from the old nine-to-five conventions, and starts to wonder what a truly modern education system looks like. His double loop learning, in other words, can carry him through his career, his entire life, expanding and enriching his experience and opening up constantly new horizons.

It's the things you *don't* see or give a second thought that most deserve your renewed attention. But when brought out into the light of conscious awareness, we give ourselves the chance to actively change things, to experiment and adjust.

It may be that the history teacher doesn't take his ideas far, or his experiment in student-led lesson plans flops. It doesn't matter, however. This would not be a failure, but simply a possible outcome from the process. The real failure – one we so often don't see or measure as one—is the unexplored alternative, or the missed opportunity to improve.

We don't think of entrepreneurship as learning, but that's precisely what it is— learning about your customer, your market, your best product. The business that barges ahead while failing to learn the lessons the customers are teaching will fail. With a growth mindset, an entrepreneur can drop their ego, start from scratch and become comfortable assuming nothing.

Those operating from a growth mindset look at every bit of information that comes to them with the same curiosity—why is this happening? What happens if I do something different? What's working? What isn't?

There are no value judgments, just receptivity. No ego, no fear of failure, no blame, no embarrassment, only a sincere desire to apply oneself consistently to the process of improvement.

At some point, make the conscious decision to *choose to value learning over being right.* Actively court feedback from others and notice how the world doesn't end if you challenge yourself or admit that something could be better. Rather, notice how dropping resistance to failure seems to bring a kind of relief, and a whole lot of open space to *play*. Take fear and ego out of the equation and you will always learn much, much faster.

- Start by asking questions.
- Become curious about your process and honest about how it could be improved.
- Conduct an experiment.
- Use what you learn to make changes, then appraise again.
- Turn experience into concrete action.

Here's how that may look in real life:

- An artist begins by asking about their assumptions about good art, how one learns better technique, and so on.

- They notice that they are merely mimicking other artists, and honestly see that their technique is lacking in originality.
- They try something new—they paint without expectation, experimenting with a process where they make art they never intend to share with anyone, just to see what happens.
- The art turns out to be surprisingly original, but the technique is still lacking. The artist begins again and commits to painting more in their own style, now asking what new techniques they can learn instead of the conventional ones they began with.
- They take concrete action—they change teachers and start studying a method that is more in line with their own style and creative expression.

Whatever your field of interest, you will likely find examples of individuals in that arena who have succeeded precisely because they chose to learn rather than to be right. The irony is that in dropping expectations, pressures, assumptions and our allegiance to old rules and norms, we give ourselves the chance to truly achieve and innovate, and at a far higher level.

Takeaways

- There are two main models of learning: single and double loop learning. Single loop learning is the way we have been taught to acquire new information all throughout our schooling years. This is the method that simply involves performing certain actions (for example, rote learning) to achieve certain outcomes (doing well in examinations). Here, the emphasis isn't on the learning itself, but the purpose for which we are learning.
- One major drawback of single loop learning is the way it handles errors and mistakes. If you make one, there isn't really a good way to resolve that besides simply doing something different (say, rote learning more effectively). We never consider the

underlying causes of our errors, instead dealing with them only on a superficial level.
- This is where double loop learning shines. It's a method of information synthesis and processing. Though harder and more involved than single loop learning, it is substantially more effective at facilitating learning. Here, we constantly utilize feedback and our own introspection to evolve the ways in which we learn. We repeatedly question the methods and steps we follow, as well as why we're following them in the first place. Instead of simply scoring well in examinations, we learn for the sake of learning, which in turn helps us generate curiosity for our subject matter. This results in holistic learning, which helps us achieve our initial goal of scoring well too.
- Those with a fixed mindset are generally more likely to learn through single loop mechanisms due to the comfort and lack of self-reflection involved. On the other

hand, those with a growth mindset are more naturally attuned to double loop learning. It is often hard to look at ourselves and accept that we may be the ones who have a fixed mindset or follow single loop learning mechanisms, but the first step to being able to learn better is to recognize the mistakes we are making in the present. This inevitably involves getting comfortable with failure, since that is unavoidable.

Chapter Three. Reading 2.0

Having considered all the various ways our behavioral and psychological obstacles can block us from learning as well as we could, it's time to turn our attention to the first practical steps we are likely to take in an attempt to learn. Whether it's a new language, technological competency, musical instrument, chapter in a textbook or entrepreneurial skill, our learning processes invariably begin the same way: with absorption of information.

Before we can begin to synthesize, manipulate, or comprehend any new data from the world around us, we need to appraise it somehow and take it in. In our world, the most common way to do this is via reading. There's a reason that accomplished people in *all* areas of life credit reading for some of their success—it's one of the most fundamentally important strategies to accessing new information.

Reading is not just reading—reading is about the skilled and focused absorption of information, to enable deep comprehension and understanding. If you think that your area of interest or expertise doesn't really require reading, think again. No matter what you are trying to learn, becoming better at reading opens new vistas and possibilities, bringing you into contact with far more ideas and perspectives than you could have encountered through direct experience alone.

On the other hand, if you read a lot already, you may not have considered how well you were reading. What could there be to learn? As it happens, reading words and understanding them is only the very first step of reading. Reading *well* is a skill in itself, and one that opens doors to many other sills. So, how do we become better at reading?

Canadian neurologist Thomas Jock Murray has explored all the ways that medical students can enrich their understanding and accomplishment as physicians, not merely by reading medical texts, but by reading widely across classical and more contemporary works and fiction. According to Sir William Osler, "To study the phenomenon of disease without books is to sail an uncharted sea, while to study books without patients is not to go to sea at all."

Great life lessons and depth of perspective usually come with being well-read. And it's not just the great classics that are relevant—students in all areas can benefit from reading graphic novels, biographies, sci-fi and fantasy stories, and popular fiction, whether the content relates directly to their chosen curriculum or not.

Those who are well-read have a breadth and richness to their inner mental landscapes that mirrors the diverse material they've encountered in their external worlds. They're better at making thematic links and connections across a range of topics, they engage more with what they read and they practice more nimble critical thinking than do people who merely stay within the narrow confines of their own discipline.

But is there really anything magical about the process of running your eyes along a page to decipher what the letters and words mean? How does this really make you a better thinker and more efficient learner?

We all know people that are smart and successful and also voracious readers—but then again, there are also many who read often but can't be said to be getting any smarter for it. What's the difference? *How* can we use the art of reading for its fullest benefits?

To actually acquire and accumulate knowledge is a conscious, active process that often takes hard work. Knowledge "absorption" is not merely passively soaking up information, but proactively working to take in data to appraise, sort, filter, engage with and critically think about the things we encounter in life.

Importantly, reading is just the tool, the method, and the conduit. To be lifelong students who constantly challenge ourselves to grow into greater mastery, we need to read with deliberate focus and conscious awareness—and this goes well beyond the page in front of you.

The billionaire Warren Buffett reportedly said, "I just sit in my office and read all day." When asked how he got so smart, Buffett held up an intimidating stack of paper and said, "Read 500 pages like this every week. That's how knowledge builds up, like compound interest." Besides Buffet, other billionaires like Bill Gates, Mark Cuban, Elon Musk, etc., all take time out of their busy days to read for several hours. If people as successful as them can find the time to read, we really have no excuse to fall back on to justify our laziness.

How many pages, books or hours have you read in the last week? Or the last month or year? What kinds of material did you read, and why? Can you actually recall any of it, and how have you grown or improved from passing your time this way? According to Pew Research, roughly a quarter of Americans have never read a single book in their entire lives. The average American reads only four books a year. Compare that with the successful billionaires we mentioned earlier, who each manage to read about two to three books every week.

Ask yourself, what new avenues are you inspired to explore? What was your strategy and intention in reading what you did? And what did you do with the knowledge and understanding you gained?

You can probably see from your answers that some kinds of reading are going to be better for your learning than others.

It matters what we read—trashy magazines, uninformed opinions or mind-numbing entertainment won't cut it.

It matters how we read—passively letting things wash over you only wastes time and opportunity.

It matters what our habits are—we don't read once, learn once, understand once. Rather, it's an ongoing *process*.

It matters what we do when we read—good reading is very much about thinking, asking questions, looking for the hidden logic, critically appraising ideas and responding with our own.

"But I don't have time to read!"

If learning is important to you, then reading should also be. And if reading is important, then it's always possible to make time.

Can you find just one hour a day that you would otherwise fritter away online, by watching TV or mindlessly procrastinating? Dedicate that one hour to reading instead. As a long-term investment that only appreciates in value, you can do no better than reading, every day. Sure, you may have to forego an hour spent working/earning, but in doing so you are probably increasing your future earning potential.

Researchers at Carnegie Mellon have found that reading actually rewires your brain by increasing the amount of white matter in your head. This has a significant impact on your ability to articulate new and interesting ideas with better eloquence.

Right, so we've explained *why* you need to read more. Let's explore *how* we can do it.

Mortimer J. Adler wrote his famous *How to Read a Book* way back in 1940, but its advice is as relevant today as ever. The first distinction we need to make is between reading for entertainment, relaxation and enjoyment, versus reading to learn, gain information or understanding. The second distinction is between reading for information and reading for understanding.

If you read something that is completely intelligible to you, you might pick up a few interesting facts, but your *understanding* doesn't increase. However, if you encounter something that originally seems difficult to grasp but upon reading it, you eventually gain an appreciation of its meaning, you have actively moved from a state of lesser understanding to one of greater comprehension. You've learnt!

As an extreme example, simply reading a train timetable or some facts about a historical battle may well leave you with more details than you had before, but you can't be said to understand more after reading. However, if you read an article explaining the deeper fundamentals of train scheduling or the broader contextual reasons for why certain historical events happened the way they did, you would gain understanding.

The downside of this is that reading challenging material will take you even more time than getting through something more accessible. So how do we find the time to do all this reading? We all have the same twenty-four hours on any given day, same as all the billionaires who nevertheless manage to fit extensive reading into their schedule. Over the years, many of them have shared the tips and tricks they use to learn and cultivate their knowledge. By making use of these tactics in our own lives, not only can we find time to read more, but retain more of it as well.

Of the many successful readers out there, Bill Gates is one figure who has been fairly liberal in sharing the tips he uses to ensure he goes to bed smarter every day. Perhaps some of his most useful techniques are these.

Firstly, he recommends writing and making notes in the margin of books. This ensures that you're truly taking in the information you're reading, as well as engaging with it to come up with new ideas. For those who can afford it, he also recommends buying multiple copies of a book, at least one paperback and one ebook, to ensure that you can read anywhere and everywhere. Even if you can't take a physical book somewhere, having an ebook ensures you can read on your phone or tablet.

Lastly, another tip that Gates and other billionaires recommend is to simply carve out an hour every day for reading. Absorbing information, especially complex material, requires your undivided focus. It isn't something you can do for a few minutes here and there. Setting aside an hour allows you to direct your attention entirely toward the material you're reading, in turn enabling you to absorb more of it as well.

Four steps to reading

While tips and tricks from billionaires can help you read more, these might well prove to be useless if you don't know how to read in the first place. The thought of someone not knowing how to read words might sound absurd, but many of us do read in ways that are either inefficient or ineffective for retaining information for long periods of time.

To aid us in this endeavor, Adler outlined four cumulative stages to reading. They are cumulative because each builds on the next—you cannot skip a stage.

Stage 1: Elementary reading (or, How to read)

This is the basic skill of understanding that the squiggles on the page mean something, and deciphering that meaning. This is the level of merely knowing what the words in front of you literally say; it's what we worked from as schoolchildren and return to if learning another language.

The nuts and bolts of language are understood and used practically at this level. Here you learn how grammar, spelling, the alphabet and various rules of vocabulary and syntax work. If you've managed to make it thus far in this book, you've already successfully completed this step.

Stage 2: Inspectional reading (or, Should I read this?)

When you scan a text superficially, you are doing inspectional reading to get an idea of the overall content and type of information to be found in that text. What kind of a novel is it? What is this blog post about and is it relevant or interesting to you? Is this the kind of thing that you want to (or indeed can) read? Skimming and scanning answers these questions for you.

- Are you reading for pleasure or for information?
- What information do you want to gain, and how does this text support your goals?
- What are you hoping to have gained by the time you finish reading?

Look at the subtitle, and blurbs on the front and back cover or inner flaps for summaries or info about the author. Decide what genre it falls into. Flip to the table of contents and look at both the chapter titles and the overall book structure. Flip through the book and look at any diagrams, the index or glossary at the back.

Can you see what other books the same author has written? If you want to, read the intro, prologue or the first few paragraphs of each chapter to get an idea of the style, tone and general arguments the author will be making. Flip through the book and read any sections that stand out to you—are they relevant, interesting or useful?

Now, don't just dive in and start reading. Depending on what you discover, decide whether you'll read the book at all, when, why, and how. You might decide to put it on a waiting list for the time being, or simply read the introduction and final chapters to get a flavor. You may instead choose to read something else before embarking on this book, or forego it entirely for something more relevant, appropriate or interesting.

For difficult texts, you may benefit from first conducting a superficial read, where you move quickly without pausing to try to understand unknown words or concepts. Read through from start to finish, understand what you can, and pass over what you can't. You can dig in with dictionaries or use external resources later; first just get a general grasp of the material, and your familiarity with it.

This method primes your brain by beginning with what you can grasp, and using that to build on and understand any new material. Consulting outside resources too early or picking slowly through a dense text can slow you down or worse, have you feeling bogged down and overwhelmed.

It's a great skill to read in an attempt to tease out the general argument in a text, even if you're not familiar with all with the details of each individual premise. Finally, avoid reading other people's opinions or commentaries about the text before you've given yourself the chance to get a sense of it on your own.

"Should I write in my books or dog ear the corners?"

Yes! Adler thoroughly believed that you need to make a book your own. A book is not a sacred object that sits pristine on a shelf and decrees immutable laws from within its pages. Make a book a part of your life by writing thoughts or questions in the margins, bookmarking important passages or highlighting and underling crucial paragraphs.

Use asterisks, shorthand symbols, colors, links to other chapters, your own opinions and arguments, and more—this makes your reading a dynamic dialogue, and not a passively received sermon! We'll look closely at note-taking skills and techniques in a later chapter.

Stage 3: Analytical reading (or, What am I really reading?)

This stage entails thoroughly picking apart your reading for the sake of deep insight and understanding of its content. Properly digesting and analyzing a book takes time and patience—and it's an active process that requires you to constantly engage with what you're reading, how it's presented, the underlying arguments, and so on.

We can break this stage down into three separate steps. The first step is an attempt to answer the question, "What is this book *generally* about?" in the least amount of words as possible. This is the step where we classify and outline the book in a broad sense, to get a rough overview into which we can then embed the details we'll learn later. Doing so also gives us a clue on this book's position relative to other books.

Ask the following questions:

- What is the genre, niche, subject or topic? (e.g. animal behavior)
- Can you state the main theme, thesis or point in one or two sentences? (e.g., It's about using positive reinforcement to train dogs for police work.)
- What are the parts, elements or pieces that make up the book? (e.g., It has an intro, a history section, then a three-part practical guide before finishing with a conclusion.)
- What problem is the author trying to solve? (e.g., The author wants to give

beginner dog trainers a comprehensive manual for K9 theory and practice.)

Though it may seem obvious sometimes, take the time to deliberately answer these questions—a lot of time and effort can be wasted on a book that is not relevant or appropriate for you, i.e. when you thought it was something it wasn't!

The next step is to ask, "What is the book saying and how is it saying it?" Again, try running through a few questions to help you understand the overall *content and style*:

- What terms, special vocabulary, jargon or keywords does the author use? See if these can be inferred from context or if there is a glossary. (e.g., you may spot "antecedent stimulus," "anthropomorphism" and "contiguity" as you scan)
- What are the major premises of the argument? These are the author's claims or propositions, or the

answers they're supplying to a question. (e.g., Traditional negative reinforcement training doesn't work. A more subtle approach is needed. There is some evidence to support positive reinforcement techniques, among others.)
- What conclusion does the author come to, and does their reasoning lead here satisfactorily? (e.g., The author claims their method works, and supplies clinical studies and also testimonials from prominent dog trainers, leading you to think the method may very well be a good one.)

The final step is one that some readers may be tempted to do earlier, but should more properly come only once we thoroughly grasp the *what* and *how* of a book's content: our response and opinion. In other words, you need to comprehensively understand what you are looking at before making an opinion or judgment on it!

It's rude to start arguing with a person before you've let them speak, so do the book the same courtesy and listen—*really listen*—to what it says first. Remember that it's also perfectly valid to withhold judgment if you feel you don't have enough information or context to say either way.

- Do you agree with the material? Why or why not? (e.g., I find the author's argument persuasive—the testimonials seem sincere and irrefutable.)
- Has the author been unaware, misinformed, illogical, incomplete or otherwise biased and unfair?

This step can be the hardest of all. Remember that your main goal is learning—not confirming your own pet theories or getting the satisfaction of being the one to hold the "right" opinion, but learning. This sometimes involves more nuanced thinking, humbleness, or the maturity to say, "I personally don't like it, but it does make a certain kind of sense."

Reading to merely confirm our own biases is no better than reading for entertainment or escapism. It may feel fun or vindicating, but will not lead to learning. As we saw in the very first chapter, a growth mindset entails being able to honestly and maturely accept when we don't understand, or when it's time to drop a clearly incorrect view.

On the other hand, if you have genuinely and mindfully done your due diligence, do not hesitate to disagree with a book's premises—even if it's a "classic" or written by a high-profile or prominent thinker.

Stage four: Syntopical reading (or, What else can I read?)

The previous stages were about taking in and understanding the book in front of us. This last stage is about reading more broadly, beyond the limits of any one single book, to consider many different books on the same topic. If you can read broadly on the same topic you give yourself the opportunity to draw creative, novel links between ideas and theories, and deepen and enrich your insight into the material, far more than if you'd merely stayed within the narrow confines of just one perspective.

Syntopic reading is about actively comparing, contrasting, and drawing a web of connections between different authors' arguments, not just linearly reading one book after another. You need to be able to assess the quality, relevance, suitability and potential bias in everything you read, and how each text fits into the bigger picture.

Can you identify the top five highest quality resources in your area of interest? What are the current main themes, controversies, unknowns and givens in this area? Who are the major players and what are the major arguments?

- You need to have a good grasp of the essence of each book or text. No single book will give you a comprehensive overview, but can you synthesize a collection of summaries from the top handful of authors?

- What terminology, concepts and ideas are common to all the texts you encounter? How do the authors use language differently, and what does this say about the content itself? Is there a historical or cultural element?
- Revisit a more general query—which questions are the most germane, now that you've read more than one perspective? What single question are *all* the authors answering?
- Can you find any points of disagreement or inconsistency? How have these interdisciplinary issues been resolved so far? This could guide further reading or lead you to input your own theory or interpretation.
- Looking at all the literature as a whole, what bigger patterns can you see emerging in the way the authors write, and *why* they write? Do you agree with their conclusions? Picture yourself at a table with the key players, having an informed conversation about the most significant themes.

As you can see, the process outlined above goes way deeper than merely picking up a random text and reading it without any focused goal or proper engagement with the material. Reading *properly* requires a disciplined effort to engage with knowledge and ideas in an intelligent way. The art of learning unfolds when we turn up to these practices with the proactive intention of gaining understanding, and not just knowledge or entertainment.

As you read this chapter, you might have wondered if books were the be all and end all of reading. What about blog posts, forum posts, the news, comics, novels, and magazines? The world is brim-full of things to read, and the internet brings an unimaginable abundance of material to our fingertips. But the truth is that quantity is never a replacement for quality, and just because something exists, doesn't mean you have to read it.

Being as spoilt for choice as the modern reader is today, discernment becomes more important than ever. Thanks to the internet, compared to the past, the publishing barrier to entry is extremely low, and today anyone can say anything—including outright lies and misinformation. A responsible reader who is committed to true learning will pay attention to the quality of what they read, and never forget their responsibility to read wisely and broadly.

The so-called "Prompt" reading criteria method can help you not only select the best material but avoid creating a "filter bubble" where you are never exposed to anything outside of what you already know. Also, you save time by not reading pointless information or unfounded opinion masquerading as fact, and give yourself more opportunity to develop as neutral a view as possible, so your own opinions are properly supported.

The PROMPT criteria for appraising texts

P is for Presentation

How is the information presented—is it laid out properly? Is it clear and succinct and can you find the information you're looking for? A low-quality presentation may not always mean low-quality information, but it could very well suggest poor organization. A neater, more concise book may suit you better if the presentation is lacking.

Example: Many "fake news" sites set themselves up to mimic more official-looking governmental bodies, but a quick look will show you that it's all a ruse—the information may be nothing more than a fringe group's unfounded opinion on the topic.

R is for relevance

When you scan and skim, does this text look like it fits your needs and goals? Is it written for you as the audience, to your needs and at your particular level of understanding? Basically, you need to understand whether the material has a chance of helping you achieve what you need to achieve. It can be a brilliant piece of writing—but that doesn't mean it will help you on your mission of learning.

Example: You may be considering reading a scholarly journal article about the efficacy of a certain agricultural technique only to realize that it was created in a completely different country with a different climate and geography. It's a great paper, it just has nothing to do with your interests!

O is for objectivity

Closely related to this is the neutrality of the information presented. But be careful—very little in life is "objective fact," even when people swear they are 100 percent bias free!

Is something being sold to you? Who has sponsored or funded the publication and why? What's the agenda? Who are the vested interests here and how do they benefit from your reading and agreeing to the text? Can you identify any "spin"?

Many people *think* they are able to identify bias, when in fact they are simply good at agreeing with those they agree with, never even realizing that the version of events they've taken in is not strictly the whole truth. Particularly if you're looking for information on politics, history, culture, matters of ethics or any controversial topics where large amounts of money are involved, pay careful attention.

Besides, many topics in these fields don't quite have an objective answer at all. There is no right answer to whether one system of ethics is better than the other, or whether a particular culture has any "advantages" over a different one. In such cases, you'll need to deliberately seek out counterarguments. Examine expert analysis from many points of view—different authors, news sites, and so on. Actively challenge your own assumptions and ask whether what you're reading is fact or opinion.

Based on your findings, form an informed opinion by yourself and continue seeking material that might potentially challenge it.

How would the issue at hand change in a different time, place or context? Critical thinking is difficult to master and requires strict intellectual standards, but you also don't want to veer into suspicious conspiratorial thought patterns!

Example: You may want to verify whether something a politician said is factually correct. However, you discover that some sources believe it to be factual while others deem it a lie. In such cases, examine the reasons behind a source's agreement or disagreement with the original statement and make your own judgement.

Method

As the name suggests, method refers to the way in which research or a given text goes about making its central point. As you read, ask yourself questions like this. Is the methodology of research clear here? Are these methods easily understandable? Was their use appropriate in the given context?

Do not assume that all published material follows sound methods of argumentation. Evaluate the texts on your own and conclude for yourself whether the method used by the author is a good one or not.

P is for provenance

The internet is a strange thing—the information appears as if by magic in front of our eyes. In the past, words deemed worthy enough to be printed in ink and read were assumed to have a certain authority; but today, words and ideas are ubiquitous. Provenance means asking *who wrote this, and why?* It means considering the source of information.

Though it's true that credentials don't automatically make an author correct or remove their biases, it's an extra bit of trust gained if an author is transparent about who they are, what their interests are, and what qualifies them to write what they do.

Opinions are opinions, but it's fair to rank more highly the educated and considered perspective of experts than those who merely have an opinion.

Here, the context also matters. You might seek only peer-reviewed journals and recent research from medical experts in trying to understand your diagnosis, but you may have a completely different set of criteria when on a support group forum that allows patients to share their personal stories.

Look at who published something and why. If you read a pamphlet about the health benefits of drinking milk, but find out that it was written by a doctor employed by a major dairy company and published by a "research group" that is really a dairy lobby in disguise, you can take the information with a pinch of salt. Such conflicts of interest are often declared by the publishing entity, so make sure to look out for those clarifications to know the intentions of an author.

Example: You may be searching for some academic material relating to a topic on social sciences that you have extremely limited knowledge of. As such, you're unaware of which authors might be well-reputed or trustworthy. In such cases, having a large number of citations is a reliable indicator of the influence of an article or paper within a particular sub-field. This is because citations indicate that others have incorporated that article into their own work, and have likely found it helpful for their own purposes.

T is for timeliness

The world moves fast. Information that is correct and fair one moment is not so a minute later. While some knowledge holds its value over the decades, other areas are developing rapidly, and you should take care to seek out information that is new and current.

For example, if the topic is the economy, the Coronavirus pandemic, the value of various cryptocurrencies, climate change or various political happenings, you'll need information that is up to date.

Be aware of when something was published and spare a thought for the fact that new information may have since emerged to make that information less valuable than it first appears. However, this still doesn't prohibit you from partaking in more general and classic material that will help you better interpret current events.

SQ3R

Another framework for getting the most out of a resource is called the SQ3R method, developed by American educator Francis P. Robinson. It is named for its five components:

- survey
- question
- read
- recite
- review

Survey. The first step in the method is getting a general overview of what you'll be reading. Textbooks and nonfiction works aren't like fiction or narrative literature in which you just start from the beginning and wind your way through each chapter. The best works of nonfiction are arranged to impart information in a way that's clear and memorable and builds upon each previous chapter. If you dive in without surveying first, you are going in blind, without understanding where you are going and what you are trying to accomplish. You should get a lay of the land first, *before* you delve into Chapter 1. The survey component enables you to get the most general introduction to the topic so you can establish and shape the goals you want to achieve from reading the book.

It's just like taking a look at the entire map before you set off on a road trip. You may not need all the knowledge at the moment, but understanding everything as a whole and how it fits together will help you with the small details and when you're in the weeds. You'll know that you generally need to head southwest if you're confused.

In the SQ3R method, surveying means examining the structure of the work: the book title, the introduction or preface, section titles, chapter titles, headings and subheadings. If the book is illustrated with pictures or graphics, you'd review them. You could also make note of the conventions the book uses to guide your reading: typefaces, bold or italic text, and chapter objectives and study questions if they're in there. In using the survey step, you're setting up expectations for what you're going to be reading about and giving yourself an initial framework to structure your goals for reading the material.

Beyond books, you should survey all the important concepts in a discipline. If you can't find it within a structure like a book's table of contents, then you need to be able to create it for yourself. Yes, this is the difficult part, but once you are able to lay all the concepts out and understand how they relate to each other at least on a surface level, you will already be leaps ahead of others. Use the survey component to form an outline of what you'll learn. In a sense, it's more like you're plotting out a metaphorical "book" for yourself.

In this phase, you'll want to determine exactly what you *want* to become knowledgeable about, as specifically as you can. For example, if you want to learn all about psychology, that's going to take a significant amount of time. It won't happen in one shot. You'd want to specify it a little more: the early history of psychoanalysis, the works of Sigmund Freud and Carl Jung, sports psychology, developmental psychology—the possibilities are plentiful.

You'll want to keep an eye out for phrases or concepts that appear in several different sources, since they represent elements that come up often in your chosen field and might be things you have to know. Draw connections and cause-and-effect relationships before even diving into any of the concepts in detail.

Question. In the second stage of the SQ3R method, you're still not diving into the deep end. During the question stage, you'll work a little more deeply to prepare your mind to focus and interact with the material you're reading. You'll take a slightly closer look at the structure of the book and form some questions you want answered or set up the objectives you hope to achieve.

In the question phase of reading a book—or, more precisely at this point, *preparing* to read—you'd go through the chapter titles, headings, and subheadings and rephrase them in the form of a question. This turns the dry title the author has given into a challenge or problem for you to solve. For example, if you're reading a book on Freud, there might be a chapter called "Foundations of Freud's Analyses of Dreams." You'd rewrite this chapter title as "How did Sigmund Freud's work on dream interpretation originate, and what were his very first ideas on the subject?" You could pencil that question in the margin of your book. If you're reading a textbook with study questions at the ends of the chapters, those serve as excellent guides to what you're about to find out.

Now that you've organized your resources for study planning, you can arrange some of the topics you're going to cover into questions you want answered or objectives you want to meet. Based on the source material you've lined up and the patterns you might have observed, what specific answers are you hoping to find in your studies? Write them down. This is also a good time to come up with a structure for answering your questions—a daily journal, a self-administered quiz, some kind of "knowledge tracker"? You don't have to answer the questions yet—you just need to know how you're going to record them when you do.

Reading. In this stage you're finally ready to dive into the material. Because you've gotten the lay of the land and formed some questions and goals for your studies, you're a little more engaged when you finally sit down to read. You're looking for answers to the questions you've raised. Another underrated aspect of formulating and organizing before you actually begin reading is to build *anticipation* for learning. You've been looking over everything for a while now, and you'll probably be eager to finally dive in and answer the questions you've been mentally accumulating.

This step is where most people try to start but fail because they lack a foundation and instead have unreasonable expectations.

Now you're being deliberate and paced about your reading so you can comprehend better. This means slowing down—a *lot.* Be patient with the material and with yourself. If a passage is difficult to understand, read it extremely slowly. If you aren't getting clarity about a certain part, stop, go back to the beginning, and reread it. It's not like you're reading a page-turner novel that you can't put down. You're reading information that might be densely packed—so tackle it slowly and attentively, one section at a time.

Chances are that reading is part of your study plan, but so might visual aids, online courses, and internet resources be. Use them exactly the way you'd use the book in the reading phase: deliberately and persistently, with the goal of fully understanding each concept you're being taught. If you get lost, remember the rewind button and scrolling are your best buddies. Plan your study time around getting as complete a level of comprehensiveness as you can.

Reciting. This step is crucial in processing the information you're learning about and is the biggest difference between reading to learn and reading for entertainment. Now that you're familiar with the material, the aim of the reciting phase is to reorient your mind and attention to focus and learn more fully as you go along. In other words, this step is about literal recitation.

Ask questions—out loud, verbally—about what you're reading. This is also the point where you take copious notes in the margins of the text and underline or highlight key points. Recitation occurs verbally and also through writing. However, it's important to restate these points *in your own words* rather than just copy phrases from the book onto a piece of paper. By doing this, you're taking the new knowledge and putting it into phrases you already know the meaning of. This makes the information easier to grasp in a language you understand. It makes it significant and meaningful to you.

If you have a geology book, you might rephrase and rewrite key points in the following way, starting from the original text:

> "This comparison suggests that the slow progress of erosion on hills and mountains is similar to the much more rapid and observable changes seen in miniature all about us."

You could rewrite the above into something like this:

> "Mountains and hills experience the same decay as happens in lowlands and rivers, just more slowly. Similar to baseball players."

What I'm doing here is putting one single bit of information into two distinct phrases, one of which I had to come up with myself. This is a huge tool that's used in memorization, and it's also a great way to make the information more meaningful to me personally. I also added a bit about baseball because I like baseball, and it makes the concept instantly understandable when I look back at it. Repeated throughout the course of a whole book, this process multiplies your learning capacity by itself.

The recitation phase in organizing your studies is great because it works across different mediums, and there are plenty of ways you can express your questions and restatements.

Review. The final stage of the SQ3R plan is when you go back over the material that you've studied, refamiliarize yourself with the most important points, and build your skills at memorizing the material.

Robinson breaks this stage down into specific days of the week, but we'll just mention some of the tactics in general. They include writing more questions about important parts you have highlighted, orally answering some of the questions if you can, reviewing your notes, creating flashcards for important concepts and terminology, rewriting the table of contents using your own words, and building out a mind map. Any kind of practice that helps you drill down, take in, and commit information to memory is fair game (though flashcards are especially effective).

This step is meant to strengthen your memory of the material, but it does more than that. It can help you see connections and similarities between different aspects that you might not have picked up at first and put concepts and ideas into greater context. It can also improve your mental organization skills so you can use this practice for other topics.

Think of this step as the natural continuation of the survey. At this point, you've gained an outline of the field, you've gotten into the nitty-gritty, and now you should take a step back, reevaluate, and make updated, more accurate, and insightful connections. Pair that with memorization, and your path to self-learning and expertise becomes essentially a shortcut. Flashcards. Mind maps. Timelines. Unanswered follow-up questions. Categorizing. Critical analysis, drawing conclusions, and asking, "If X, then what follows or precedes it?"

The SQ3R method is no joke. It's exhaustive and detailed and will take patience and sharp organization to pull off. But if you give yourself the patience and devotion to take each step seriously and slowly, you'll find it incredibly helpful to tackle a complex subject. And each time you do it, it's a little easier than the last.

In explaining the SQ3R method, we briefly skimmed the role of organization and notes and how they impact self-learning. After all, you can't organize everything in your head only and hope to be effective.

Takeaways

- Reading is undoubtedly the best way to gather new information on any given topic. Each subject has tons of written material dedicated to it; we just need to find the resources that most closely sync with our motivations behind studying a particular topic. Yet, even if we

discover these resources, how do we read in a way that helps us retain the most information? How can we maximize our learning through the written word? The first step here is to just take some time out to read from our busy schedules.
- Mortimer Adler has outlined four distinct steps that describe how exactly we should read in order to derive the most benefit from it. If you're reading this, you've already completed the first step, which is learning how to read. Following that, you need to learn how to identify resources worth reading. This can be done by skimming through parts of a book and seeing whether it appeals to our interests. Once we find some suitable books, we utilize analytical reading, wherein you closely analyze what it is that you're reading. Figure out the main thesis of your book, what genre or category it falls under, the historical context of the author's arguments, etc. Lastly, read several different books on the same subject

and compare the arguments they present in what is known as syntopical reading.
- When it comes to selecting the best reading material, follow the PROMPT technique. This stands for Presentation, Relevance, Objectivity, Method, Provenance, and Timeliness. Consider all of these factors and evaluate resources based on them. Each refers to an aspect of different resources that make them worth considering.
- Finally, the SQ3R method for extracting information from a resource. Use it. It stands for survey, question, read, recite, review. This is not just a process for attacking a book, but rather a plan for tackling entire disciplines and fields—and whatever you are trying to learn for yourself. Most people will use some elements of the SQ3R method, such as the read and review portion, but without the other elements, deeper comprehension is rarer and more difficult.

Chapter Four. Just Ask

Have you noticed the parallels between fixed and growth mindsets, and the attitudes one can have toward reading?

Fixed mindset: reading is simply for amusement or to confirm what I already know. I avoid anything challenging or which pushes me out of my comfort zone. I already basically know everything I need to anyway.

Growth mindset: reading is a powerful way for me to engage with my world and all the ideas and perspectives within it, and I am constantly doing it so I can learn more. I don't mind being wrong or not understanding something on the first try—that's what learning's for!

As we've already mentioned, learning that comes from a place of fear or control is seldom true learning, whereas the attitude of open-mindedness and curiosity is the heart of deep insight into the world and its mysteries. And what is the best tool for the curious mind? That's easy: a question.

Children are notorious for asking tons of questions. The average child asks anywhere between one to three hundred questions every single day. However, as they (and we) grow up, the number reduces to only about six questions per day. Somewhere along the way, we lost the natural curiosity for life that we had as kids.

As many parents know, children often ask questions that are deceptively simple, yet extraordinarily hard to explain in simple terms. This is because they force us to reconsider many of the things we have learned to take for granted over our years of existence. If we retained or managed to rebuild the same curiosity we had as children, the rate at which we would learn would accelerate enormously.

The famous quote from esteemed theoretical physicist Heisenberg goes, "What we observe is not nature itself, but nature exposed to our method of questioning." The right question will give us the information we want. The wrong question will keep us circling around at the level of the problem, never rising above or outside it.

A question allows us to draw out the information we want from our surroundings, to interrogate it, to understand it more deeply, to learn. This is the intelligent receptiveness that is alert to the new all around us.

In fact, intelligence on its own is not all that important—raw processing power alone is not very useful. Rather, it is our wise ability to know what we know and don't know, to understand how to find out information, to not merely be geniuses from the start but to determine how to grow and learn from where we are—these are the attributes that make the difference.

It is not the skills we're born with or the resources at our disposal, but the efficiency with which can use what we have. Indeed, this is the growth mindset again: it is not where we are or what is fixed in us, but our ability to move and develop beyond that. After all, another way to look at growth is to call it… learning.

As you read, pause to respond to and engage with what you encounter using questions. Ask open rather than closed questions—for example, ask "What are all the current communist states in the world and what's their history?" rather than "Is Vietnam a communist state?" or "Exactly how is this thing operating?" rather than "Does it work?"

Open questions expose you to a wealth of new information that you may not have been aware of. However, in some cases, closed questions can be useful in getting answers to particular queries. Being able to ask highly specific, detail-oriented questions is also a skill in itself, one that might lead you to right answers more efficiently depending on how you use them.

As you read, stop occasionally and question yourself to check your comprehension. When we learn in school, our teacher plays this role for us, using questions to guide our understanding and to reveal any gaps in our knowledge. As autodidacts (people who teach themselves), you can employ a lot of the techniques used in education on *yourself*.

Ask, in effect, "What did I just read?"

It may be helpful to imagine yourself re-explaining the concept to someone else—a good test to reveal if you truly grasp the principle. Being the teacher for a moment highlights all the steps, stages, and assumptions you need to make to arrive at your conclusion.

Ask what you *don't* know. Ask where the author/teacher/expert gets their information from and why they're doing what they're doing. Ask what assumptions both you and the author hold. You get the picture: ask a lot of questions, and when you get an answer, question *that* even further!

Rather than judging the veracity of the text in front of you, or jumping in to decide whether you agree or not, try first just to describe and understand what you are reading. Hold off on evaluating, and simply become curious about what is presented and how.

Read again, slowly. If you're having a lesson with someone, you can do the same. Ask questions to hone in on the errors or assumptions you may have. Remain in the growth mindset by looking at the task rather than how well you're doing it, and let go of any assessments you may have about your performance.

If you fail, look at the failure square on and ask it questions, too: What can you teach me? Why did it go the way it did? What if I tried it another way?

When learning anything (a sport, the piano, a new game, lines for a play, a lab technique, difficult programming language or whatever), you want to go beyond the realm of facts. Ask questions, but questions that probe for *insight*. Remember, you are not keeping score, competing or appraising yourself. You're learning. A question is simply a tool that helps learning—and it needs to be a sharp, effective tool.

A good question is one that illuminates misunderstanding or ignorance. It guides us out of confusion, or at least shines a light on the reason for our confusion. A good question breaks things down so we can see more clearly. By slowing down and "thinking aloud," we make it easier to catch our assumptions or errors. We open up a space for more insight to flow in—or at least more creative questions.

Questions for thought

Let's consider a few kinds of good questions, and how to ask them. The first is **Elicitation**. These questions check for the presence of knowledge and ask who, what, when, and where.

For example:

Who was the UK's prime minister in the 1930s?
What's the full chemical name of this particular molecule?
Where can I find the fuse box on this model?
When does the sun set?

Divergent questions are another kind, and expand and open up your thinking process. These questions will help you compare and contrast two situations, sort out a seeming discrepancy or inconsistency, or highlight differences and distinguishing features. The essential characteristic of this type of question is that it never has a specific "right" answer, unlike when it comes to convergent questions. These are more likely to be why and how questions, as these are more open-ended and open to analysis and flexibility.

For example:

Why does this dog training method work for breed A, but not really for breed B?
What is the fundamental difference between these two authors' positions on this topic?"
How does the television work? Is it magic?

Elaboration questions open up the field of information even further and expand on what's known, to gain more complexity and richness. Simply asking, "what else?" will lead you to elaborate and deepen not just your comprehension but likely your recall, too. "Can you tell me more about this?" is the perfect open-ended elaboration question. Think about this as zooming in on a topic.

More examples:

Are there any other techniques associated with this printing technique?
Exactly how does this part of the engine actually work?

Clarification questions highlight crucial details and add definition. These are great to ask when we have just discovered a gap or error in our thinking. Clarification questions can often clear up misunderstandings or reveal assumptions.

For example:

Why exactly do we calibrate the machine that way and not the way I just did it?
Why am I assuming XYZ, and is it true?

Heuristic questions are those that query your method of problem solving directly, and not the content of your thinking per se. These can be incredibly helpful if you're stumped on a problem. These questions all directly help you improve your method of questioning.

For example:

How would I know I've gathered enough information on this topic?
Am I missing anything in my process?
What would I do if I was an expert in this area?

Finally, **inventive** questions are those that spur creative, out-of-the-box thinking by asking your brain to run wild with concepts and connections. These can be powerful methods to abandon stale old assumptions and open the way to a fresh new solution or way of looking at things.

For example:

If I was a caterpillar, why would I decide to build my cocoon here and not somewhere else?
What would I say to a younger version of myself when it came to this issue?
If our synchronized swimming team had a personality, what would it be and why?

Sometimes, you might merely need to read a text more than once to find answer to questions right under your nose. Other times, you need to read "between the lines" and try to get an overall sense of what is being said across paragraphs and chapters (and indeed, what isn't being said!).

Some questions will require you to use a blend of what you're reading and your own prior experience and knowledge, while others will be 100 percent about your own opinion and response to what you read. You might imagine that you are a teacher trying to discuss or teach the topic to a class, or a prosecutor in a courtroom, asking pointed questions to unravel the truth.

Whatever you do, always be making *connections*:

How does this sentence connect with the previous one?
How does this paragraph fit into the rest of the chapter and the whole book?
How does this book measure up against others like it and in the field at large?
How does this book square with your own experience and ideas?

How does this topic relate to other topics?
How do all of these topics fit into the world right now?
What about the world as a whole, including all of history and the future?

Queries both deep and superficial can help you answer these questions and make these connections.

A single text that you read and comprehend is great. But why not introduce your newly found ideas to all your old ones! See how it fits into the toolkit you already have, and become curious about new combinations. You may even find that you can use these fresh new ideas to replace some outdated or frankly terrible ones you had before.

So many people read one-dimensionally. We can blame our education system for this, since most students are taught to read fixed texts in very fixed ways in order to answer fixed questions, only to win marks and get grades to level up through their schooling career.

But when you self-teach, you need to expand your thinking as wide as possible. In real life, there *simply are* no discrete subjects, divided up with neat, clean boundaries, one hour per each study period on a neat timetable. There is no fixed curriculum, with deadlines for assignments and exam dates and a team of teachers ready to use a rubric to grade your answer. This is a good thing!

Read what's in front of you, but read everything that's around it, too.

Become curious about the author's attitude and intention. In formal or academic texts, for example, the authors can go to great lengths to present their views as fact. But if you dig a little you can soon see that this kind of formal language is a mask to conceal very ordinary human motivations—to appear smart, to argue a passionately held opinion, to justify a (probably irrational) emotion or to make a case for how things should be rather than how they actually are.

Dig deeper. What style is the author using and why? What does this say about them, about you, and about the topic at hand? Why might a person seek to distance themselves from their writing by using stiff, passively constructed sentences and dry Latin terms? On the other hand, why would the author consistently use second person and address the reader like an old friend? Is the author making any assumptions about *you* as they address you from the pages?

Often, authors will assume a degree of familiarity with certain concepts on the part of their readers. These concepts might not always be apparent, since they can be denoted using words that we ordinarily use to mean something else. Stay on the lookout for such references for maximum learning.

What cultural, historical, economic, religious or political context is informing your author's claims? You might rightly question the validity of an account of what it was like to be a woman living five million years ago, not least because the author is not a history expert and is a man to boot.

Reading well is a little like a good conversation—it's equal parts "listening" and "speaking," and flows along with respectful curiosity (on both sides!). You might like to keep a journal to help you deliberately write out questions that occur to you as you read. Pause after each paragraph to let what you've read settle and congeal.

A great habit is to pause after each chapter or section and try to guess what is coming next in the author's argument. A well-written book will address your issues, concerns and questions as they naturally emerge in the flow of the book, but take careful note if this doesn't seem to be the case.

Are any knowledge gaps yours or the author's?
What don't you understand and why?
If you're struggling to understand, how else can you approach the idea or topic? What other resources are available?
Can you identify any bias?

How might the author's writing be influenced by who they are, where they're from, how they've been educated, their interests, etc.?

How does what you've read match up with other authors? What do the discrepancies mean?

Putting aside the content itself, has the author made a clear and coherent argument that is logically sound?

What is the author not including, and why?

Finally, the biggest question of all: How does what you've read address any of your stated goals in your own learning journey? What concrete knowledge, wisdom or skills can you take from having read it?

Close your loop by deciding on some real action to take, inspired by your reading. Maybe you pick a book from the reference list and read further. Maybe you read a little about the author themselves, or choose another author who has written more recently. Or, maybe you decide to throw the book in the trash and move on (it happens).

All this question asking, however, is not just for the texts you're reading or the information you're encountering. It's for *you*. To the extent that you can practice multi-dimensional, flexible and proactive thinking about your own process, the faster you will learn and the deeper your comprehension will be.

Regardless of what your chosen area is, what your goals are or where you are in your level of skill, make a habit of routinely asking yourself questions to guide and deepen your learning:

- Do I really understand the deeper underlying mechanisms for the process I'm trying to learn or master?
- What is the quality of my study material like—is it complete, accurate, up to date?
- What psychological and behavioral obstacles are standing in my way of better learning, and what can I do to remove them?
- How effective, in general, are my attempts at learning so far?

- Can I be honest about those parts of my process that are not working for me?
- How has my thinking process changed and developed so far? What do I want to do more of and less of, and why?
- Am I able to put things in my own words, explain concepts to others, summarize, analyze, apply concepts, connect, deduce, create, evaluate? Which skills need more development?
- Am I doing enough to support my creative, nonlinear thinking?
- Do my routines support a growth or fixed mindset?
- Is it time to consider a completely new perspective, or expand my current one?
- Who do I admire and who could I learn from?

Sometimes, we won't be able to figure out the answers to questions we ask ourselves. In such cases, it is imperative that we seek help from others. Many of us hesitate to ask for help out of a fear of appearing dumb or incompetent, but asking and engaging with others is an integral part of learning. Even if we don't have a particular person we can rely on to answer our questions, there are other resources we can utilize.

Post on online forums about your queries; there are bound to be dedicated groups based on the skill or topic you're trying to learn about. Though we can learn well enough by ourselves, engaging with others provides us with perspectives that we might never even have considered. Asking others questions online or in person gives you an opportunity to do just that. Once you receive satisfactory responses, don't forget to question them too!

Socrates the great

The importance of being a question master cannot be overstated; it's not about being pedantic or provocative. We've said multiple times that you can't expect information to teach you or to make itself understood. This responsibility will always fall upon you in the end. If you're not getting or understanding something from a lecture, book, or video, the answer surely cannot be to keep reading the same passage over and over.

You must make an effort to investigate and pull understanding out yourself. It just makes you think of psychology experiments where rats continue to shock themselves by pressing a lever. No progress is being made, so obviously the approach needs to change. It's a clear example of working smarter, not harder; no one can deny that the rat works hard, but with questionable results.

Let's consider two people who read the same book on Spanish history. Jimbo will read along and review the information. He will take notes and can pass a test quite easily on the subject. His answers read like bullet points for a recipe for cornbread. He receives a B+. Kudos for Jimbo.

Kunal, on the other hand, reads the same book, but he only does this once or twice, and instead spends the rest of his time trying to gain a deeper understanding of the whys and motivations of Spanish conquistadors and kings. He attains an A+ on the same test, a better mark because he displayed a deeper insight than Jimbo could ever possess. His answers are more like essays, and even though he forgot a couple minute details, he made insightful leaps of reasoning and judgment because of his deeper understanding.

He achieved this level of mastery by asking probing questions and using them to get behind facts and information. He processed the information and chewed on it with his questions. He finds that he doesn't even need to know all the facts if he asks the right questions, because he can predict what the conquistadors would probably have done. Kudos for Kunal.

In learning, it is said that answers are far less important than questions people ask. Indeed, we've also heard this advice in relation to job interviews, where you should always have "intelligent questions" to display that you understand the interviewing company on a deeper level.

Rote memorization of information is sometimes the goal, but if we ever want to understand and comprehend more deeply, questions are the first place to start. Questions will take a flat piece of information and turn it into a living, three-dimensional piece of knowledge that interacts with the world at large. That is the reality of any fact or piece of information; it has a story we are usually overlooking in the interest of speed or efficiency. To ask a question is to see a subject, identify what you don't know, and also be open to the fact that your entire understanding could be wrong. Meaningful learning only occurs when you understand what surrounds information, such as the background and context.

Put another way, good questions end up allowing us to *triangulate* understanding. Take a textbook, for example. It is necessarily broad and cannot hope to cover all the subtleties involved. If we fully accept what we read, then we are set on a singular path. If we ask questions, we are able to see that the path itself contains twists and turns and may not even be accurate. Different lines of inquiry are generated, and it is understood that there are multiple paths, each with their own perspective. Questions allow us to both clarify misunderstandings and reinforce what we already know. In the end, we come to an understanding of the same textbook that is nuanced and more accurate.

Luckily for us, teachers have known this for literally thousands of years. The most helpful framework for generating insightful questions comes from no other than Socrates himself, the ancient Greek philosopher perhaps best known for being Plato's teacher, as well as being executed by the state for "corrupting the minds of the youth." His method of teaching was largely in the form of dialogues and questions, appropriately called the *Socratic Method*.

When you boil it down, the Socratic Method is when you ask questions upon questions in an effort to dissect an assertion or statement for greater understanding. The person asking the questions might seem like they are on the offensive, but they are asking questions to enrich both parties and discover the underlying assumptions and motivations of the assertion or statement. It is from this process that we have a framework for effective questioning.

Imagine that you make a proclamation, and the only response you get is a smug, "Oh, is that so? What about X and Y?" Unfortunately, the know-it-all questioner is on the right path.

American law schools are notorious for using the Socratic Method. A professor will ask a student a question, and then the student will have to defend their statement against a professor's questioning regarding the merits of a case or law. It's not adversarial by nature, but it does force someone to explain their reasoning and logic—and of course, gaps in knowledge and logical flaws will probably surface. This process serves the goal of deeper understanding and insight. It may cause defensiveness, though it is not offensive in itself.

So what exactly is the Socratic Method, beyond asking a series of tough questions that make people uncomfortable? When you do it to yourself, you are forcing understanding. You are putting yourself through an incredible stress test that will make you question yourself and your logic. It will force you to discard your assumptions and see what you might be missing. If you are mercilessly questioned and picked apart with Socratic questioning, what remains afterward will be deeply comprehended and validated. If there is an error in your thinking or a gap in your understanding, it will be found, corrected, and proofed with a rebuttal. That's deep learning.

As a brief example, imagine that you are telling someone that the sky is blue.

This seems like an unquestionable statement that is an easy truth. Obviously, the sky is blue. You've known that since you were a child. You go outside and witness it each day. You've told someone that their eyes were as blue as the sky. But remember, our goal with questions is to better acquire knowledge as to the sky's blueness. So imagine someone asks *why* you know it is blue.

There are many ways to answer that question, but you decide to say that you know the sky is blue because it reflects the ocean, and that the ocean is blue, even though this is erroneous. The questioner asks how you know it is a reflection of the ocean.

How would you answer this?

This brief line of Socratic questioning just revealed that you have no idea why or how the sky reflects (or doesn't) the blue of the planet's oceans. You just attempted to explain an underlying assumption, and you were mildly surprised to discover that you had no idea.

That, in a nutshell, is the importance of the Socratic Method. A series of innocent and simple questions directed at yourself, honestly and earnestly answered, can unravel what you thought you knew and lead you to understand exactly what you don't know. This is often just as important as knowing what you do know because it uncovers your blind spots and weaknesses. Recall that it was used by teachers as teaching tool, so it is designed to impart deeper understanding and clarify ambiguities.

There are six types of Socratic questions as delineated by R.W. Paul. After just briefly glancing at this list, you might understand how these questions can improve your learning and lead you to fill in the gaps in your knowledge.

The six types of questions are:
1. Clarification questions—why exactly does it matter?
2. Probing assumptions—what hidden assumptions might exist?

3. Probing rationale, reasons, evidence—what proven evidence exists?
4. Questioning viewpoints and perspectives—what other perspectives exist?
5. Probing implications and consequences—what does this mean, what is the significance, and how does it connect to other information?
6. Questions about the question—why is this question important?

Clarification questions: What is the real meaning of what is being said? Is there an underlying hidden motivation or significance to this piece of information? What do they hope to achieve with it? Suppose we have the same assertion from above, where the sky is blue. Here are some sample questions from each category you could plausibly ask to gain clarity and challenge their thoughts.
- What does it matter to you if the sky is blue?
- What is the significance to you?
- What is the main issue here?
- What exactly do you mean by that?

- What does that have to do with the rest of the discussion?
- Why would you say that?

Probing assumptions: What assumptions are the assertions based on and are actually supported by evidence? What is opinion and belief, and what is evidence-based fact or proven in some other way? Unless you are reading a scientific paper, there are always inherent assumptions that may or may not be accurate.
- Is your blue my blue?
- Why do you think the sky is blue?
- How can you prove or verify that?
- Where is this coming from exactly?
- So what leads you to believe the sky is blue?
- How can you prove that the sky is blue?

Probing rationale, reasons, and evidence: How do you know the evidence is trustworthy and valid? What are the conclusions drawn, and what rationale, reasons, and evidence are specifically used in such a way? What might be missing or glazed over?

- What's the evidence for the sky's color, and why is it convincing?
- How exactly does the ocean's reflection color the sky?
- What is an example of that?
- Why do you think that is true?
- What if the information was incorrect or flawed?
- Can you tell me the reasoning?

Questioning viewpoints and perspectives: People will almost always present an assertion or argument from a specific bias, so play the devil's advocate and remain skeptical about what they have come up with. Ask why opposing viewpoints and perspectives aren't preferred and why they don't work.

- How else could your evidence be interpreted, an alternative view?
- Why is that research the best in proving that the sky is blue?
- Couldn't the same be said about proving the sky is red? Why or why not?
- What are the potential flaws in this argument?
- What is the counterargument?

- Why doesn't the sky color the ocean instead of the other way around?

Probing implications and consequences: What are the conclusions and why? What else could it mean, and why was this particular conclusion drawn? What will happen as a consequence, and why?
- If the sky is blue, what does that mean about reflections?
- Who is affected by the sky's color?
- What does this information mean, and what are the consequences?
- What does this finding imply? What else does it determine?
- How does it connect to the broader topic or narrative?
- If the sky is blue, what does that mean about the ocean?
- What else could your evidence and research prove about the planet?

Questions about the question: This is less effective when you are directing this question to yourself. Directed toward someone else, you are forcing people to ponder why you asked the question or why you went down that line of questioning, and realize that you had something you wanted to evoke. What did you mean when you said that, and why did you ask about X rather than Y?

- So why do you think I asked you about your belief in the sky's color?
- What do you think I wanted to do when I asked you about this?
- How do you think this knowledge might help you in other topics?
- How does this apply to everyday life and what we were discussing earlier?

At first, it sounds like a broken record, but there is a method to the madness. Each question may seem similar, but if answered correctly and adequately, they go in different directions. In the example of the blue sky, there are over twenty separate questions—twenty separate answers and probes into someone's simple assertion that the sky is blue. You can almost imagine how someone might discover that they know next to nothing and are only able to regurgitate a limited set of facts without context or understanding.

You can apply the Socratic Method to ensure that you are understanding what you think you are understanding. You can think of it as a systematic process of examining and just double-checking yourself. The end result will always be a win, as you either confirm your mastery or figure out exactly what is missing.

Suppose you hear from a friend that the Spanish Inquisition was a fairly humane process of light interrogation, with only minor maimings and lashings (various sources put the death toll at, on average, around one hundred thousand people). In this instance, you can use the Socratic questions to correct a mistake. The six question types, as a reminder:
1. Clarification questions—why does it matter?
2. Probing assumptions—what hidden assumptions might exist?
3. Probing rationale, reasons, evidence—what proven evidence exists?

4. Questioning viewpoints and perspectives—what other perspectives exist?
5. Probing implications and consequences—what does this mean, what is the significance, and how does it connect to other information?
6. Questions about the question—why is this question important?

To check the veracity of this statement, you might ask:
- What exactly is being said, and why does it matter?
- What is that statement based on?
- What makes you think it is true? Where's the evidence for it?
- Who might have this perspective, and why? What might be the opposing perspective? Why is that?
- What does this mean for Spanish history as a whole? Are all history textbooks incorrect? What else will be affected by this knowledge?
- Why do you think I might be asking you about this?

What about using the Socratic questions for deeper understanding of a topic, such as the biology of the brain? Actually, the questions don't change—all six of the above questions can be used in the same way to more deeply understand brain structures. You'll learn, you'll poke holes, and you'll understand. Isn't that what this whole thing is all about?

Takeaways

- As children, we once asked hundreds of questions a day to satisfy our natural curiosities. However, as adults, we increasingly refrain from expressing our doubts out of fear of appearing stupid or from a tame acceptance of things as the way they are. However, asking probing and relevant questions is the best way to aggregate answers that challenge our preconceived notions and foster expansions of knowledge. The best questions expose our ignorance and assumptions about the world that didn't have any concrete basis, forcing us to think in new and better ways.

- To ask better questions, we must be aware of the different types of questions that exist. We have elicitation questions, which are used to answer "how," "why," "what," "where," etc. We also have divergent questions, open-ended queries that don't have a specifically right answer. Next, we can utilize elaboration questions to seek more information about something by asking "what else...?" type doubts. Clarification questions, as the name suggests, aim to resolve any potential misunderstandings or wrongly held assumptions. Heuristic questions focus on the method of questioning that we are utilizing over their content. Lastly, inventive questions are radically creative questions that can be used to juxtapose one piece or information with another through analogies or comparisons. This helps us understand complex concepts

through the knowledge we already possess.
- Ask questions about anything and everything related to your subject matter. From the author's intentions, to the idiosyncrasies of his or her writing style, the motivations behind making certain arguments, the methodologies the author uses, and everything in between, all of it is worth putting under the scanner.
- Another helpful framework for questions comes from Socrates. He put forth a set of six types of questions for critical thinking, deeper understanding, and peeling back the layers of just about anything. These types of questions include: clarifying, probing assumptions, probing reasoning and analysis, probing viewpoints and perspectives, probing implications, and probing the question or assertion itself.
- If we fail to answer our questions ourselves, there is no shame in seeking help. Make use of online forums that are dedicated to the

topic you're trying to study. They likely exist—you just need to find them.

Chapter Five. Notes as Your Second Brain

We've considered the obstacles to learning, and the best mindset and approach to learning in general. We've looked at how reading is a key practice for anyone wanting to learn anything, and we considered the various ways to read better.

But have you ever read something, understood and even agreed with it, only to have it float completely out of your mind just a few days later? The world is a big place and filled with plenty of interesting ideas—many of which we risk losing if we don't have a system for *recording* them so we can return to them later. Memory is a wonderful tool. But note-taking is perhaps handier, and a practical way to externalize our own memory so that our brainpower is freed up to do more creative, analytical and problem-solving thinking.

By taking (smart) notes we allow ourselves to process, recall, organize and collate information as we learn and acquire knowledge. Notes are like the written expressions of our inner thoughts—by putting our thought processes down on paper we in effect capture them, as well as give ourselves the chance to inspect them and rearrange them as needed. None of us can be said to have learnt anything if we cannot easily access all this new knowledge or insight.

What comes into your mind when you think of taking notes? Are you picturing school or university days where you quickly scribbled along in a notepad as the teacher talked? While there's nothing wrong with this technique, there's much, much more to note-taking as a discipline in your ongoing learning. As you may have guessed already, optimal note-taking is not something that happens by accident; you need a *system*.

The Luhmann method

Prominent 20th-century sociologist Niklas Luhmann designed a note-taking system so appealing that many continue to use it today. Luhmann understood (perhaps inspired by his sociological training) that *context* mattered more than *content*. Context is the bigger picture: the network of relationships surrounding any one piece of information. Essentially, the system entailed creating separate index cards for each idea, which connected them to as many other ideas as possible. The idea was to thematically link ideas to one another as he assembled these cards into what he called a "slip box"—something like a second brain that synthesize novel associations and insights.

He began by writing an interesting idea on an index card and numbering it. When a new piece of information was added to this, he would subdivide the subsequent index cards, for example 1a, 1b, 1c, etc. Branching connections could spread infinitely in all directions, and could themselves have their own branches. Each card would forever have a permanent ID number that would identify it and its place in the tree of ideas. Ideas with longer and more complex reference numbers were those that had a greater history and had been more thoroughly explored.

If this decentralized, potentially infinite labelling system has you thinking of hypertext and the structure of URLs, it's interesting to note that the system predated the internet. But Luhmann must have done something right, as the prolific work he created using this system was well-received and certainly novel. Luhmann created an astonishing 90,000 notes during his life (around six a day). He even claimed that the box had a sort of life of its own, and that he in effect established a dialogue with it—all by virtue of not relying on his own brain to remember properly and make novel connections.

What can we learn from Luhmann? You don't need to replicate his system exactly to benefit from the underlying principles. Let's take a closer look.

Principle 1: note-making is not an outcome, but a process

Don't take notes to record what you have already thought about, but to assist you in expanding your thinking. There's a reason your old schoolteachers always wanted you to paraphrase texts in your own words—in writing these notes, we are in effect seeing them for the first time, from the inside out, and have a far better chance of comprehending and remembering. Think of taking notes as another medium for thinking, using pen and paper rather than your mind.

When you take notes, you pick apart data and gain a deeper understanding. By elaborating, translating, reordering, questioning, comparing, contrasting, rephrasing and explaining, we dissect an idea and truly begin to understand it. The truth is that, no matter how smart you are, this is difficult to do mentally. You can get more done by externalizing your thought processing and working with it in the form of notes.

Principle 2: write as though you had an audience

It doesn't matter if your notes or ideas are ever published or read by another human being. What matters is that you practice discernment in what you note and how. Don't waste time on things you know are trivial; be rigorous, focused and demand quality from yourself. Picture these notes being read and relied upon in future. Avoid vagueness and repetition, and make your words count. When you are deliberate, conscious and purposeful in your note-taking, your thinking will follow suit and you will learn more quickly, and with deeper understanding.

Furthermore, focus on your presentation, especially if you prefer to write your notes instead of using an electronic device for them. You might take notes meticulously and efficiently, but if the information isn't presented in a comprehensible manner you will refrain from relying on them in the future. Making your notes aesthetically pleasing can do much to increase the amount of information you retain from them.

Principle 3: creativity doesn't happen in a void

You can't form opinions unless you understand the topic, and you can't create something completely new from scratch. You can't find any interesting answers until you've taken the time to research interesting questions. In other words, learning/studying is not so very different from creating.

When you take notes, you are having a conversation with the supporting course material. You don't have to pluck things from thin air. Every bit of understanding rests on some prior bit of understanding—so if you're trying to solve a problem or create something new, don't start from nothing, start with what you know.

Famous physicist Richard Feynman had a technique that involved him writing in a notebook called "Things I don't know about" and actively shaping his learning efforts around figuring those mysteries out. This is a simple but profoundly useful note-taking/journaling technique that keeps your focus where it should be, and allows you to use what you know to find out what you don't know.

Allow fresh patterns to emerge. It's a non-linear process—there's no reason you can't return to old notes and elaborate. Extract key information, shake it up or try putting it in a different format. When notes are done well, you'll be able to use them as milestones on your way to learning, or as a scaffold that helps you inch closer and closer to understanding using baby steps along the way.

Principle 4: have a standardized workflow

While the note-taking part of the process is flowing and open-ended, you still need a structured protocol for how and when to take notes. If you're committing to reading an hour a day, add on ten minutes so you can jot down notes, questions and reactions. Try cut down on distractions and clutter and focus on extracting the essence of what you read to create beautiful notes.

You might like to re-read these notes as you continue reading the same or another book, and add to or amend them as you go. Keep it simple: if a "slip box" doesn't serve your needs, you don't need to have one. Try bullet journaling, mind mapping, or a system of your own creation. What matters is that it *works* for you.

Make sure that your notes, whatever form they take, are uniform. You need something in a standardized format that you can compare and carry over across any and all topics and books.

Principle 5: regularly appraise your process

It's a trap to get too attached to any one method or technique and lose sight of the fact that it's not really working for you. Note-taking is an iterative process: make sure you constantly ask how well your process is going, and refine as you go. The design and implementation of a note-taking strategy itself must be open for adjustments. You'll know your notes are beneficial if they inspire fresh ideas, reveal connections you wouldn't otherwise think of, motivate your curiosity and creativity, and help you keep track of a complex, "bigger picture" idea that would have eluded you if you'd just approached learning in an ad hoc way.

Ask questions like:

Do you ever return to your notes?
If you do, how do you use them? Is your method working?
In what ways can your notes support your learning? Could you do better?

Make notes of progresses made, insights gained, knowledge banked and leading questions that will help inspire the next step of your learning. Use notes to self-assess, record points of challenge or areas to focus on, criticisms, unknowns, issues, inconsistencies. Note down your plans, your intentions, your methods and your success. Make lists. Check them twice. Your notebook is a scratchpad where you tackle these aspects of your learning process in a dynamic and intelligent way.

Principle 6: The more the merrier

Don't have separate notebooks for separate disciplines or projects – combine them. Work on many learning projects at once and "cross-train your brain" by reading several books at once, considering each in the context of the other, to get a broader view. The more ground you cover, the more likely you are to stumble on a happy "accident"—an idea that suddenly illuminates your topic for you, or advances your understanding.

As you make notes, remember to keep them diverse and interesting. Bounce ideas off one another, and don't limit yourself to one book, one idea, one author, one field. The best *aha!* moments are often those that find us by surprise—but we can certainly lay the foundation for them. You might glean information from a book about politics to use in your psychology class, or you may organize some new skills according to the projects you hope to use them for, not in their conventional categories.

Principle 7: Keep it interesting

It's a rule of learning that the more personally relevant and interesting a piece of information is, the greater your chances of understanding and remembering it. To care about what you're learning, to really grasp it, you need to have a clear and direct line to your own self-determined goals. You need to feel like the information fits into the bigger picture of your learning.

When we're trying to learn something new, we can sometimes lose our enthusiasm as we get bogged down in the technicalities and details. Try often to use questions and curiosity to re-engage your passion for your topic. Remind yourself of why you're learning in the first place. Make sure you're directing your *own* learning process, and not merely slaving along with someone else's idea of what your growth should look like.

As Luhmann famously said, "I only do what is easy. I only write when I immediately know how to do it. If I falter for a moment, I put the matter aside and do something else." What is "easy" is what feels natural, obvious and interesting in the moment. Learning seldom happens by force or rote. Gather information and be diligent, but know that insight and understanding can't be forced or faked. Follow your genuine curiosity, interest and passion and you will never feel unsure or unmotivated.

The Ahrens' method

Inspired by Luhmann and his principles, Ahrens published the book *How to Take Smart Notes*, to help people create notes that they could use to write articles or books. For our purposes, we can use Ahrens' method to create study notes and materials that consolidate and encourage our learning.

Step 1: Pause frequently as you read to ask questions and make notes, *in your own words*, either in a notebook, on index cards or using the method of your choice. You may even like to use a note-taking app like Zotero to keep it neat and quick. These are called "fleeting notes" and don't need to be complex or organized. They're primarily to jog your memory and help you catch the gist of certain fleeting ideas.

Step 2: Create permanent "literature notes." These should be "atomic" (on just one topic), permanent (you'll never change them), self-contained (understandable even out of context, weeks from now when read again) and concise (keep it simple). Literature notes are essentially conceptual breadcrumbs—remember to include some bibliographic details and be selective about what you keep as a note.

Step 3: Link literature notes together. Here's where the magic happens. You need to see all the ways you can connect your note with other existing notes. Some people claim that the true effect of note-taking requires patience, and only kicks in once you have around 1000 notes. Note down the relationship between this note and others—does it support, contradict or expand on them? Without this step, notes are just scribbles—they mean nothing.

Some tips on creating notes that will work hard for you:

- Use abbreviations when possible (you may need to create your own abbreviations list until you get the hang of it)
- Use concise terms when possible, and create shorthand for common words (for example "w/" for "with" or outing a small "20" inside a Capital letter C to signify "The Twentieth Century")
- Use color to categorize (for example red for something you disagree with or something incomplete, or different

colors for different subjects or projects)
- Consider using note-taking apps and software if it works for you (don't worry too much if it doesn't! Pen and paper work just as well). In fact pen and paper might well be better. Ahrens quotes a study in his book where students' learning was compared based on whether they use physical or digital notes. The study found that while typing speeds up the note-taking process, it does so at the expense of learning and retention. This is because when we write, it is impossible to note down words we hear or come across verbatim, forcing us to translate some of the material in our own words. On the other hand, typing makes it easier to take notes without thinking, thereby reducing how much information we retain.
- If you're a more visual learner, use stickers, decals, doodles, mind maps or artistic elements to help you

> quickly grasp the essence of a card or note at a glance.

- Keep things simple! You don't necessarily need a system of note-taking as elaborate as the one Luhmann followed. The important thing is to be able to rely on your notes to understand the topic(s) they cover while also allowing you to bring notes on different sub-topics together.

In sum, there are eight main steps you need to follow if you want to build an efficient note-taking system like Luhmann's. We've already covered the three different types of notes that are going to be a part of this method: fleeting, literature, and permanent notes. The first three steps involve making these notes in the aforementioned order.

Let's say you're trying to study ethics and you're reading a book that lays out the two dominant strands within this topic, deontological ethics and utilitarianism.

Your first step is to create fleeting notes based on your first impressions of what these two concepts are. So, you could write that "deontological ethics points to any ethical system that has certain fixed rules, for one reason or another" and that "utilitarianism is the ethical position which says that all moral considerations should be based on which action provides the maximum benefit to the most people involved."

You might also make a third fleeting note that carries an example you made up yourself to illustrate the difference between the two, like the infamous trolley cart dilemma. As you can see, these aren't formal definitions of these systems, but rather informal characterizations of them.

Next, you must make literature notes based on relevant information you come across related to these two ethical models. Select only the most important quotes that you find, and rewrite them in your own words using as few words as possible. On the back of your note, write its bibliographical source for future reference. To use our example, this might be information related to the most important thinkers on both sides of the aisle and why they have chosen the side that they did.

For your third step, you'll be combining the information in your fleeting and literature notes to make permanent notes. Of the three, these are the ones that'll actually make their way to your slip box or note chest. To make effective permanent notes, consider the content of your other notes and relate them to the reason behind you wanting to learn about, in this case, ethics.

The goal here is to develop strong arguments based on what you read. As such, while compiling permanent notes, look for inconsistencies or contradictions in your subject matter. For instance, once you're familiar with utilitarianism, you might realize that a utilitarian will happily oppress and subjugate individuals or minorities if doing so serves the larger interest. Do you think that is justified? Why or why not? As questions like these pop into your mind, use different notes to take them all down separately. You can now dispense with the fleeting notes and literature notes, although Luhmann himself collected his literature notes in a separate slip box.

Here is where, depending on your propensity for note-taking, things can get slightly complicated. Once you've arranged your permanent notes in the slip box, you'll want to create an index note. This fourth step is optional, but will help you connect different notes in a way that makes studying complex topics easier. Your index note is essentially a table of contents that contains keywords related to your topic.

To take our example, you could have an index note with just two keywords, utilitarianism and deontology. Write the keyword on top of permanent notes that relate to these particular keywords and arrange them in an accessible way. One good idea might be to use different colors of notes or ink for different keywords. The length of your index note is entirely up to you, so use as many keywords as you think you might need.

Once you have your index and permanent notes in place, you're done with the note-taking part. Now, you need to extrapolate information from your notes and put them to good use. Go through your permanent notes to discover ideas and interesting arguments that might serve your purpose behind learning ethics.

You may also choose to turn your notes into a single manuscript for coherence and ease of access. To do this, you'll need to connect all your permanent notes to form a coherent argument about why, say, one system of ethics is better than the other. As you discover holes in your own argument, try to fix them as best as you can. Finally, edit and proofread your manuscript to get rid of any mistakes that might have escaped your notice.

Takeaways

- Being able to read large amounts of text is of no use if we don't have an effective way to remember the information we come across. Our memories are not capable of retaining everything we read, and so we need an efficient system of note-taking to aid us in remembering as much information as we can.
- Not only does note-taking help us remember more by writing important concepts or ideas in concise and easy language, we inevitably engage with our content in creative ways when we assemble information in a systematic manner.
- The sociologist Niklas Luhmann devised a system of note-taking that is still held in high regard decades after its genesis. Besides his elaborate system itself, there is much to learn from the way Luhmann treated note-taking. This includes treating note-taking as a process that facilitates new and creative ideas instead of simply being a repository of those we have already thought of.

Taking notes demands a standardized workflow that must be followed to maximize productivity. We must also treat our notes as if they are going to be presented to an audience. This encourages us to compile them in a manner that is aesthetically and logically appealing enough to be revisited for future reference. The more notes we make, the better. As long as we have an efficient way to sort them, they are bound to be helpful to our purpose of learning. As we make more and more notes, we must also regularly appraise our progress and rectify any errors that might have previously escaped our notice.

- Other useful tips for making effective notes include using abbreviations and shorthand to minimize the amount of space taken by words and denotations. Using different colors to highlight or mark unique sub-topics also aids us in accessing specific concepts within vast, complex subjects. Having said that, keep things as simple as you can. You don't need an elaborate note-taking system if a minimal one does the trick.

Chapter Six. Lessons from the Science of Learning

What helps you learn better is what helps *you* learn better. Depending on what you want to learn, why, your strengths, weaknesses, goals, context and skill level, your optimal technique may look nothing like someone else's. That said, there are definitely a few general principles behind most successful learning methods that are backed up by research.

Most of us are familiar with the same handful of standard study techniques from school or university, such as spaced repetition (gradually increasing the time between a stimulus and a learnt response, for example with flashcards) or all the different methods that come with deliberate learning (i.e. sitting down at a set time and place to learn something very specific).

Some study techniques really work, while others merely give the illusion that you know more than you do. The following four principles cover a range of different techniques. As you chart your learning path, try to include as many of these as possible, in a way appropriate to your topic.

Technique 1: Self-explanation and purposeful elaboration

Many prominent thinkers have expressed a common sentiment over the years: if you cannot easily explain an idea to a five-year-old, then you don't truly understand the concept. A 2014 paper in the journal *Memory and Cognition* by Nestojko et. al. explained how "expecting to teach" improves a person's ability to retain and organize new information. Trying to explain what you have learnt to a real or imagined audience is helpful, but it may actually be the anticipation of having to teach in the future that forces your brain to adopt a particularly receptive and focused state of awareness.

The researchers' study was simple: students asked to learn a passage in order to complete a test later on performed worse than students asked to learn the same passage specifically with the intention of teaching it to someone else. The latter students were better able to recall main points and details, and the information they retained was better organized.

The trick may lie in adopting a more active stance to what you're taking in. How many times have you read a paragraph, eyes glazed over, scanning the words on the page but not really taking in any of their meaning? Expecting to teach may prime your mind and get you to read more actively, looking for key points and clues to important information. As you read, your brain is already actively assembling a mini-curriculum in your mind.

There are variations on this principle. "Elaborative interrogation" is the act of making a thorough explanation for why a certain fact is the case. Investigated by educational psychologist Michael Pressley and colleagues since the mid-'90s, this technique has plenty of promise as a way of learning details and facts—even confusing ones. Rather than merely learning what is true, you force yourself to explain the reasons for it being true. By slowing down and asking your brain to truly understand, you bypass the need for rote memory and retain the concept at a deeper level.

Importantly, this doesn't just mean accessing and memorizing an explanation, but creating one yourself; it's the *process* that enables better understanding. What's great about this is that the more prior knowledge you have, the better this method works, because you have more mental "scaffolding" to build on when learning something new.

This technique may entail nothing more complicated than regularly asking "why?" Sometimes we think we understand something, but when asked to outline it clearly (literally speaking it aloud, if possible), we reveal to ourselves the gaps in our knowledge. If you get something right, explain how you arrived at your answer, or think about how you would outline the process for a fellow student. By understanding the steps and method, you give yourself a better chance of repeating them in future when you solve a similar problem.

Self-explanation is a related technique, and also depends on the most available resource you have: the things you already know. Self-explanation uses prior knowledge to explain and understand new knowledge. Rather than approaching any new data from scratch, you try to anchor it and contextualize it to what you already understand.

Many of us practice the technique without even knowing it, but it's something that we can certainly take better advantage of. The effectiveness of this method depends heavily on the content and the degree of your prior knowledge. It's best combined with other techniques and approaches.

A simple way to bootstrap new knowledge using old knowledge is to make analogies. If you're an expert cook trying to learn a complicated laboratory technique, you might draw parallels between the two, imagining the lab process as a "recipe."

Even creating a summary can be said to draw on this same approach to learning, provided you are crafting the summary in a spirit of extracting the essence of a concept to share with someone else, i.e. to teach them. Some people find it enormously helpful to imagine they are teaching themselves as they learn. This can be combined with questioning or creative note-taking.

A person learning a new musical piece on an instrument might notice themselves struggling on a particular section. They slow it down, take it apart and look at it more closely. They imagine themselves explaining to others *why* this piece is so difficult. By elaborating this way, they understand what needs to be learnt—a new fingering pattern, a different position of the hands, etc.

The person might then coach themselves mentally as they go: "*Hm, that didn't seem to work so well... why do you think that is? Take a look at the position of your fourth finger. You already know that in the previous piece you learnt, the fourth finger can sometimes be a problem with this technique... OK, sit up straight and try again, breathe deeply and pull your fourth finger away on the third count, like this...*" They trial and error a new approach, engaging and responding dynamically to their own learning, rather than mindlessly repeating the same pattern over and over without getting anywhere.

Another way to improve your self-explanations is to use concrete examples while trying to learn. Let's go back to the discussion of ethics we used in the previous chapter while learning how to effectively take notes. We can use the classic example of dividing a cake between three children to illustrate the principles we learned of. The deontologist would divide the cake based on some preconceived rule such as "everyone gets equal parts." However, the utilitarian would say that we should divide the cake to maximize the total happiness derived by the division. So if one kid is hungry while another is full, the former gets more than the latter.

This is just one example, but you can utilize several different ones to help self-explain different ideas to yourself. If you can, discuss your examples with others to gain feedback or constructive criticism. Alternatively, if you have access to a teacher, verify your examples with them to ensure that you've implemented the principles they're meant to convey accurately.

A recent study at the University of Waterloo found that the dual action of speaking and listening to yourself recite content helps you retain information much better than reading or writing in silence. This is because saying things out loud has a deeper impact on your long-term memory. You might initially feel slightly awkward talking to yourself, but that is a small drawback of an infinitely helpful technique. The following method of reading out loud will doubtless prove beneficial in your learning endeavors:

1) While reading your notes or subject material, underline any key concepts that you deem to be important.
2) Once you finish doing so for all your notes, go back to everything you underlined and read each concept out loud slowly, and as many times as you feel is necessary.
3) After finishing this, take a three-minute break. Following the break, cover your underlined concepts and test yourself to see how well you were able to memorize them. Testing yourself after being exposed to new information has been shown to improve recollection in the future,

making this step particularly important.
4) Repeat the above steps for any concepts you weren't able to memorize.

Technique 2: Variety is the spice of information absorption

Another well-researched and documented approach to learning can be summarized easily: mix it up!

William E. Hockley found in a 2008 paper in the *Journal of Experimental Psychology: Learning, Memory and Cognition* that the environmental context of learning has a big impact on recall and quality of understanding. Basically, if you are constantly shifting your study environment by moving locations, you give your brain more material to work with in creating memorable associations. While it's true that you want your study area to be free of distractions and clutter, you can provide your brain with more easily recalled stimuli by changing where and how you sit, the direction you face, the room you're in and so on.

You're also more likely to make connections, remembering, for example, that you learned XYZ when on the sofa that rainy morning, and ABC the following day outside in the sunshine. You remember it more easily because you can recall the sound of the birds at the time, and the feeling of the deck chair against your legs. It's not quite a photographic memory, but it brings you closer to the moment you first learnt the material.

As you study, switch things up and involve as many senses as possible: gentle, varying music in the background, a different beverage or snack each time, some incense one day and a hot water bottle the next… These are all cognitive breadcrumbs to help you find your way back to the learned material.

What about the "Mozart Effect" or the claim that listening to Mozart during study will somehow improve recall? Plenty of research has been done into the effects of different kinds of music on learning, some of it conflicting. If you're trying to concentrate hard and memorize, silence may be best, so it might work to have white noise in some earphones if you're in a place where traffic, coughing and sneezing, or random noises could interrupt your flow.

Research by Nick Perham and Joanne Vizard in 2011 indicated that music during study can increase attention and memory and boost mood—but it doesn't really matter what style of music that is. Generally, not-too-loud music without lyrics at a steady beat can boost concentration. Choose something pleasant but avoid anything you like *too* much, as this could become distracting and actually worsen performance!

Much of the effect of including elements like music or varied environments while learning has been put down to the feeling state induced by such things. When our brains are flooded with dopamine and we are relaxed and calm, we are more likely to be able to focus and learn. To this end, you might choose to include a meditative practice or other pleasing ritual into your study plan.

Just a few minutes of meditation done before you embark on your learning can encourage calmness, clearing away anxious thoughts and rumination so that you are better prepared to begin study with a clear and receptive mind. A 2016 study done on Taiwanese university students by Ho-Hoi Ching and colleagues showed that taking a semester-long mindfulness and meditation course improved both the attention and memory of the students.

This is no surprise to anyone who has tried to learn anything while stressed, low on sleep, depressed or distracted. If your brain is constantly running off in all directions and distracted by its own chatter, there's far less mental energy available for focusing on learning what's in front of you. In addition to helping to quiet your mind, meditation can support emotional self-regulation, strengthen your body-mind connection and connect you to your overarching goals and intentions for learning.

The brain is a complex thing; it doesn't operate linearly like a computer, and sometimes the connections it makes don't follow the logic they "should." However, you can take advantage of your brain's natural creativity, plasticity and connectedness. Use mnemonics, analogies, storytelling or jokes to help cement ideas in your memory—the more colorful, outrageous or even rude the association, the more you're likely to remember it.

Add dimension and flavor to your learning so you have more nodes to draw connections between. If you're learning about a certain historical period, listen to the music of that era while you study, imagine soap-opera-like dramas between the key characters and relate them to your own friends and family. You might even find movies and TV shows that are set in the same era, and watch them to help yourself visualize that era better. Create mind maps, comics, doodles, songs or puns to help link ideas together.

By using emotion and variety, you give your brain a richer and more dynamic stimulus—if you only remember *one* thread from this complex patchwork, you can pull on it to more easily recall the entire thing. Relate information back to yourself, back to emotive or personally relevant topics, back to the context you're studying in, to anything that means something to you. Your brain will always remember and prioritize things that appear to be more pertinent and meaningful.

Finally, consider "interleafing," which some research has suggested is more effective than learning in fixed "blocks" where you study only one type of problem at a time. Interleaved practice essentially means you mix up study materials, problems tackled and methods in a single study session. For example, you don't merely read through a chapter on one algebraic operation and then complete a practice run of twenty problems using that operation, but rather practice a range of problems of different kinds.

This may work best if you first study in blocks to become familiar with the basics, but as soon as you're able, start mixing things up to encourage more nimble problem solving—i.e. teaching your brain not only to solve problems, but also to recognize the difference between different problems and how to solve them. It's a little like a dynamic CrossFit training day rather than a session that focuses solely on one muscle group.

Countless studies have proven the effectiveness of interleaving for better critical thinking, more accurate problem solving or diagnosis, improvements in sports such as baseball and basketball, memory associations, math and foreign language acquisition, to name a few. Research by Doug Rohrer et. al. in 2015 showed that interleaved practice benefits math learning more than conventional practice in "blocks," and Sean Kang from Dartmouth College has written an entire book on how interleaving can improve motor skill acquisition, metacognition and recall in a wider range of areas.

Technique 3: What you do when you're not learning

Your brain is a part of your body, and your learning approach is a part of the rest of your lifestyle. Effective lifelong learners not only have study and work protocols that do the job, they also have habits and practices *outside of study* that indirectly support their learning.

The idea that physical wellness has a direct and measurable effect on cognitive health is by now well established. Regular exercise has a host of benefits, not least of which is boosting blood flow to the brain, providing fresh oxygen and nutrients to this precious organ and simultaneously removing waste products. A study done by Dr. Douglas B. McKeag concludes that a workout before study leaves you feeling more alert and focused, ready to absorb new information.

Mental training games and puzzles are great, but you may be able to derive more from basic exercise like going for a jog or swim. Exercise elevates mood and cuts stress levels, too, helping you live a more balanced and healthy life when you close the books for the day.

In 2011, a team of researchers led by Justin S. Rhodes, a psychology professor at the Beckman Institute for Advanced Science and Technology at the University of Illinois, found that mice that exercised performed better on cognition tests and had overall healthier brains. A lack of exercise couldn't be mitigated by an enriched and stimulating environment or access to toys and games—mice that didn't exercise performed worse cognitively, no matter what other enrichments they had in their enclosure. The conclusion is tentative but compelling: physical exercise makes you smarter.

A 2011 review by Kirk Erikson et. al. showed that exercising actually increases the size of the hippocampus and thus improves memory, as well as increasing what's called a brain-derived neurotropic factor, a molecule that actively encourages the growth and repair of brain cells. Exercising also releases a cocktail of mood-boosting hormones that regulate mood and energy levels.

It doesn't matter what exercise you opt for, only make sure you get your heart rate up and *move*! Many people report slogging away at an obstacle in their work or studies, only to have a flash of insight into the problem the moment they step away from the books and go for a run, for example. If you're routinely making self-care and your own fitness goals a priority, you'll build a solid routine and a strengthened sense of self-determination and confidence in yourself—which will naturally carry over to your learning activities.

If you're wondering whether other lifestyle factors—such as diet and stress—make a difference, it's no surprise that the scientific evidence strongly suggests they do. An often-overlooked aspect of healthy living is sleep, especially if you're cramming for an exam or pulling an all-nighter.

Your brain is an organ like any other in your body, and it needs to rest. During sleep, the brain recuperates and refreshes itself. Sleeping consolidates what you've leant, helping the brain retain new information. Without enough good-quality sleep, learning is measurably affected, your mood dips and your memory takes a knock. In fact, staying up all night can damage your learning ability by up to 40 percent, according to sleep scientist Dr. Matthew Walker at the University of California, Berkeley. It can take days for your brain to recover from sleep deprivation.

If you're trying to cement new ideas and strengthen your recall of new material, sleep is your best ally, and *not* cramming and staying up late into the night. Sleep done before you study primes and prepares your brain, and sleep done after study is like clicking the "save" button on your memory. Think of memories gathered throughout the day as, in Walker's words, "raw and fragile," only becoming set and solid after a good night's sleep.

Non-REM stages of sleep are deeply restful and lay the groundwork for good learning the next day. The REM stage is more active and may play a role in creatively linking new ideas and recognizing novel patterns. A good night's sleep can have you waking up to a new solution to a problem or a creative new angle to explore. It can also help you process your emotions, enhancing your ability to self-regulate and manage stress.

If learning is important—not just for the exam tomorrow but for your lifelong enrichment—then sleep is nonnegotiable. The best techniques combined with all the willpower and passion in the world will not make up for a tired brain that needs rest.

As you plan a learning strategy, don't forget to include all the activities that surround and support your learning. Routines that contain some room for flexibility are best. Eat well, sleep deeply and regularly, and exercise often to ensure that you're physically in the best position to learn to your fullest potential.

Meditate—stress can induce corticotropin-releasing hormones into your body that actively hinder the formation of new memories, not to mention making you feel awful. Regular study breaks to exercise, relax, practice mindfulness or sleep can have a better effect overall than merely ploughing on with a punishing learning schedule.

If we have not only a growth mindset/beginner's mind but also self-compassion and patience, we set more reasonable goals and don't beat ourselves up when we make mistakes, thus ensuring our path is not high-stress and unpleasant, but slow and steady. Remember, you have to continually adjust expectations according to where you're at *today*, not to where you want to be in a year's time.

What about all those special brain-boosting dietary supplements? Is it possible that certain foods, minerals or herbs can enhance your learning and even intelligence? Unfortunately, there's little consistent evidence that any of these supplements help all that much. While correcting a nutritional deficiency is likely to improve overall cognitive function, there are sadly no brain superfoods on the market that are proven to boost your concentration or any other abilities that aid learning.

However, one practice that does improve concentration and is backed by research is performing deep breathing exercises before a study session. The Trinity College Institute of Neuroscience has found that deep breathing regulates the level of noradrenaline in your brain. This neurotransmitter enhances concentration levels by calming your mind, allowing it to stay focused on one thing—the material you're about to study.

If you're confused about which breathing exercise to perform, here is a simple one that will do the job. Think of it as the "4-2-4 rule" to make it easier to remember. First, close your eyes and take a deep breath through your nose for four seconds. Once you feel that your lungs are completely filled with air, hold your breath for two seconds. Finally, exhale for four seconds. Repeat this at least thrice before studying to relax yourself.

While this exercise is best performed on a bed, make sure that you don't end up studying at the same spot. It is extremely important to separate the spaces where we study and rest. This will help our mind associate one place with one specific activity, enabling it to perform that task better. In other words, if you use your bed only to rest, you'll find it easier to relax and fall asleep when you lie down. However, if you use it to both rest and study, the opposite will likely happen. Studying on beds also comes with the considerable temptation of taking naps. Avoid it by using a desk instead!

Regardless of where you study, however, it is also important to regulate the temperature of your environment if possible. Researchers at Cornell University have found that the optimal temperature for performance is somewhere between 22-25 degrees Celsius (72-77 degrees Fahrenheit). Temperatures lower than that resulted in decreased output and more frequent errors among officegoers who were part of the study.

Lastly, time your learning schedule appropriately. Certain times of the day are better for cognitively intense tasks compared to others. Late mornings (around ten a.m.) is the time when our brain is most equipped to deal with mentally challenging tasks, whereas the time between twelve and four p.m. is when we're usually exposed to the most distractions in our day. This distinction occurs because late mornings are when our brain is the most alert, well-fed, and unfettered by the rest of the day's happenings.

Technique 4: Perfect practice makes perfect

You probably already know that rote learning doesn't work. Simply reading and re-reading through notes doesn't do much to enhance your retention. Repetition can be helpful, but not when done mindlessly and without engaging in the ways we've outlined in previous chapters.

So, does that mean "practice makes perfect" is not true? American football coach Vince Lombardi famously updated the old adage to, "perfect practice makes perfect." In other words, repeat the actions you want to master; don't cement unwanted behavior or information by repeating the same mistakes over and over. You are what you practice most—so don't teach yourself how to make mistakes, in other words!

It's easy to see this principle in action in things like sports or playing a musical instrument. But what exactly does perfect practice look like to you and your goals? Start with the fundamentals. Break down skills, new pieces of information or processes and make sure that you can perform or recall each one before trying to do the same with the bigger chunk.

Once you've mastered that, assemble a few simpler units and practice them together. If you make a mistake, stop, slow down and go back to the fundamentals. Try again later, but don't keep on and on hoping that with enough attempts you'll simply blast through any obstacles or misunderstandings.

As before, ask questions. Become curious about why something is difficult and address your efforts there. Switch things up if necessary. Later, when you're comfortable, you can up the challenge level. Be careful of prematurely taking on more challenge than you're ready for—this seldom inspires you to learn faster and can often backfire, leaving your confidence shaken and teaching you some bad habits along the way.

Consciously seeing your study or learning efforts as a practice shifts your focus from outcomes and onto how you can continually be better in process. Don't worry about becoming a virtuoso, or even finishing this piano piece. Only pay attention to this small section, to this melody, to this few seconds in front of you. Don't become too reliant on practicing the things you can already easily do. If you find yourself plateauing, you need to up the challenge.

Some skills will benefit from patient and diligent practice, and some skills will require you to focus on thinking smarter rather than harder. The only way to know what your practice demands of you is to regularly appraise and update your methods, being honest about what works. At the same time, a practice is for the long haul—improvement won't happen overnight, but in sometimes imperceptible degrees.

If the skill you want to develop or the knowledge you hope to acquire doesn't lend itself well to learning in increasingly challenging chunks, then a great way to practice is by testing yourself. It may seem a little old-school, but it makes sense: you will perform better on a written test if your practice is to complete many different versions of that test rather than make endless mind maps or notes.

If you go for this method, however, be proactive in your approach. Use the test itself as a form of questioning and appraisal of your process thus far. A good trick is to deliberately tease out the material you most struggled with and focus on that—even bringing your full awareness to an error and understanding why you made it improves your chances of not making it next time round.

How well do you know the material? What gaps in your knowledge has the test revealed? How did you actually perform under "test conditions"? These questions will make sure you're learning in a way that actually matches the end goal of doing well on that test.

For academic and memory-based learning goals, testing has been proven to lead to better retention. A 2006 *Perspectives on Psychological Science* review article by Roediger et. al. explains the "testing effect," which is a favorite research topic of cognitive psychologists. To put it simply, in most cases, practice tests boost recall and memory.

Why should that be? There have been suggestions that what is being practiced in this case is *repeated retrieval*—i.e., deliberately asking your brain to go and fetch a previously stored memory. Retrieval-based learning practice may seem basic and old-fashioned, but it has proven effectiveness when it comes to meaningfully retaining information.

Retrieval practice is best done as soon as possible after you learn a new fact or piece of information. The first time you encounter a new word in a second language, for instance, quickly repeat the word, then quiz yourself later at various intervals to give your brain the chance of retrieving that memory. This way, you are practicing the skill you want to develop—the act of retrieving the piece of information you have stored.

Another technique is to close the book, and quickly tell yourself what you have just read. Not only will anticipating having to do this prime your mind for more focused reading, you'll give yourself the chance to actually cement the memory right off the bat. This is in turn can deepen your understanding of all subsequent steps, meaning that when you do finally combine all the separate elements, they'll come together more smoothly and with more lasting comprehension.

Try past papers or practice tests if you're writing a school exam or similar, or set up conditions in which you can do a practice run that closely mimics the final goal you're working toward.

A final word on what NOT to do

In reading the above four techniques, you might have wondered why some other seemingly great techniques were omitted. What about all the methods you were taught at school? In truth, there is no single method for every student and every topic.

What is likely to be most effective is a mixed approach that is tailored to each student and their own needs—an approach that can be adjusted and tweaked along the way.

However, there are certain techniques that have definitely gathered evidence for being less than useful. These are those old habits we default to without thinking, and they can sometimes do more harm than good. If you revert to any of these methods, you may find yourself wasting time and energy that could have been better used to learn more efficiently.

Re-reading important texts is seldom useful. We've seen that reading is most effective when done with focused purpose. Read without a strategy and your brain has no reason to retain anything. Better to read fewer times but with more focus than simply read the same content over and over.

Similarly, highlighting as you read has not been shown to enhance learning. It's little more than a habitual action, and can even trick your brain into thinking that by highlighting, the material is somehow "banked," and can now be forgotten. If you've never actually gone back to look at, compile or organize highlighted sentences from a book, you have positive proof that doing so serves little purpose.

Another pitfall to avoid is getting bogged down with overly complicated note-taking strategies or learning methodologies. If you're spending more time learning the learning method than the material itself, you may be dealing with a solution that is more complex than the problem it's meant to solve, and worse, confusing or overwhelming yourself.

It's counterintuitive, but try not to overlearn. Your brain can only do so much—forcing it past its natural limits won't make you smarter, or help you learn faster, It will only exhaust you and make it *harder* to learn. Avoid cramming information in, multitasking or flitting around with material and techniques that are really only acting as distractions.

Finally, take with a pinch of salt any far-out claims of "learning styles" and how you need to convert material into your unique and preferred method of learning. The truth is, there's very little evidence that human beings have different learning styles. It was once suggested that learners could present with a predominantly visual, auditory or even kinesthetic learning style. But a comprehensive report in the *Psychological Science in the Public Interest*, a journal of the Association for Psychological Science, presents randomized trials that show there really isn't any difference between visual and auditory learners.

The review's many prominent authors found that the evidence for different learning styles was often weak or contradictory, and that there is no real reason to drastically change the format of your learning. Some learners find audiobooks and material more pleasant and convenient, but don't expect a miraculous boost in intelligence, memory or critical thinking simply because you used a more exotic learning model.

Technique 5: Use dual coding

When you're learning something new, text is important. Images and diagrams are also important. But something magical happens if you can *combine* both text and imagery in your learning materials or notes. The dual coding technique entails combining multiple modalities (i.e. text and images) to gain a deeper understanding about the concept than would be possible with just one or the other.

The dual coding theory of cognition was first put forward by University of Western Ontario's Allan Paivio in 1971. The general idea is that information can be represented in different ways, i.e. verbally or visually, and that these different modes actually use separate cognitive channels, resulting in different mental representations of the same information.

Essentially, there are *two* main memory systems in the brain, and using both simultaneously improves learning.

"Coding" is how we access, store and process concepts, but it's also how we retrieve them later. If we code a concept twice—as a verbal *and* visual piece of data, for example—we give ourselves a greater chance of retrieving that memory later on than if the data had only been coded one way.

The theory has plenty of scientific evidence to support its claims. Brain imaging techniques (MRI and PET scans) can show where brain activity occurs during particular tasks and stimuli, and reveal the distinct neural pathways associated with visual and verbal processes. Dual coding is a technique that takes advantage of the way our brains naturally work.

With dual coding, the whole is greater than the sum of the parts. For example, you might be trying to learn about a complicated physics or biology concept, of which there are several text descriptions and a diagram showing the process. The text and the image do connect to one another, but you have to do the extra cognitive work to figure out how.

If the text and image are combined, however, the relationship between them is clearer and more obvious—so you can more quickly and readily access the fundamental concept. The key is to create your own combined study materials, and to keep it simple at first so as to reduce overwhelm.

By representing one single concept or idea both visually and verbally, and making clear the connection between them, it's as though you give your brain more "handles" by which to grasp the concept. Dual coding improves your comprehension and your memory. However, there are a few tips to keep in mind:

- Make sure that the images added are actually meaningful and relate to the text. There is no gain to be had in

merely adding a picture, and you may unnecessarily add to the mental load.
- Make sure you take the time to mentally integrate both verbal and image data, by exploring the way they mutually explain and support one another. You are not merely creating a picture with some text, but a combined stimulus that tells you more than either modality can in isolation.
- Try combining this technique with your general note-taking system to save space and be more concise.
- Start simple and then add to your study materials as you go. An anatomy diagram, for instance, will be easier to integrate and understand if you begin with the most fundamental labels only.
- Think of how you can condense verbal information using visual clues. Your diagrams don't have to be realistic—they only have to capture and demonstrate key relationships, functions, processes or ideas. A chemistry diagram, for example, can

be a mix of chemical equations with little diagrams of the shape of the molecules.
- You can start with either text or imagery. If you are comfortable with a text description, try elaborating on it with imagery, and vice versa.
- If you have trouble understanding a topic, switch modality—reading a confusing description may make more sense if you try to visualize some imagery to accompany it, and a complicated diagram may be clarified with the careful addition of some explanatory text.

Investigations done both by Paivio and other researchers have shown that recall of verbal information is better if paired with related imagery—whether real or imagined. Other studies have shown that it's easier to remember concrete topics than abstract ones, with the implication that making abstract concepts more concrete will lead to better understanding and recall.

Finally, in 1969 Paivio also suggested that participants not only processed visual information separately from verbal information, but that verbal information was superior when it came to remember sequences.

"Isn't this the same as learning styles?"

Despite its enormous popularity in the education sector, the idea that different students have different learning styles (i.e. visual, verbal, auditory or kinesthetic) has not been scientifically proven at all. Thinking that some material is simply not for you may actually limit your learning potential as a student, and lead you to believe that you are simply not cut out for certain subjects—which is not true.
This "neuromyth" goes to show just how unhelpful it can be to rely on theories that only *seem* to make sense. It seems logical to imagine that people differ in learning style just as they do in personality, but the most effective approach can sometimes run counter to our intuition.

Dual coding is not quite the same as the learning styles theory, and does have considerable scientific backing to suggest its efficacy. Rather than the brain preferring just one modality, it appears to learn best when presented with rich information encompassing several different modalities. This is not surprising when you think that the brain evolved to serve us in a complex, interconnected world that speaks to all our senses at once—life itself doesn't arrange itself in neat, simplified categories!

Though it's true that different people will certainly have different preferences and personalities when it comes to learning, it may be more useful to think of the topic itself, and the style of learning it would most benefit from. It's hard to imagine learning salsa or heart surgery from a book, and just as hard to think of how you'd teach complex calculus *without* a book.

Some of the perceived benefits of the learning styles theory may actually be hidden benefits of dual coding—not merely presenting information in different forms, but presenting it in more than one form simultaneously.

"My topic really cannot be represented visually, though..."

It's easy to imagine many scientific or mechanical topics being suited to visual representation, not to mention intrinsically visual areas like art or design. But what if you're learning about something like literature, history or a new language? Can dual coding still work?

The answer is yes—"visual representation" needn't be just a picture. You can use more abstract visual elements like tables, flowcharts, timelines, outlines or other graphic organizers to represent information. Again, however, this needs to be meaningfully done: the structure and layout needs to say something useful about the text.

For example, you could use a spider diagram or table to chart out the main components of an essay, and show how each idea relates to the others. Or you could use arrows, shapes and even colors and symbols to illustrate certain ideas and link them together. A timeline or cause-and-effect diagram can lay out chronological events.

It can be a little trickier with some subjects than others, but what's important is the effort that goes into the production of such combined visual/verbal study aids. In creating these diagrams yourself, you give your brain the chance to see information from a completely different perspective, consolidating your learning. It doesn't matter too much *which* modalities you use, or how, only that you are combining them in meaningful ways that actually enhance your understanding.

"Can dual coding only be done using words and images?"

According to Paivio's original theory, yes. But perhaps we should take a closer look at what he meant when speaking about "words and pictures." Firstly, "analogue" codes refers to any codes that strongly resemble the thing they're representing.

For example, a near exact copy of a circuit diagram or a photorealistic picture of the anatomy of the skin—i.e., what we might think of as pictures.

"Symbolic codes" are representations of words, and don't map exactly onto the phenomena they're describing. These symbols are arbitrary—for example, the squares on a calendar don't really have anything with the days or months they are meant to represent. So, although words are a part of the model, they can also include symbols, numbers, variables, letters or combinations of letters, etc.

Words and images (and diagrams, symbols, etc.) are the only two modalities supported with scientific evidence.

There is some controversy about this, but it's likely that the theory would not apply to, say, auditory or kinesthetic codes. While it may prove useful to try, the key is still to form solid and meaningful associations *between* the two modes, and this may prove impossible for modes other than words and images.

Having said that, there are actually four modes of *encoding*, which is to be distinguished from dual *coding*.

When we talk about encoding, we are talking about the process of creating a new memory, and this is a term that is specific to the creation of memories. There are four types of encoding: visual, semantic, elaborative, and acoustic. The first two we've already discussed with regard to dual coding, which means that elaborative and acoustic encoding are additional ways in which to better learn.

Acoustic encoding relates to sounds and their role in memory. This type of encoding relies on something known as phonological loops. Earlier, we discussed how saying things out loud helps us retain more information, and part of the reason behind that is phonological loops.

As we repeat concepts to ourselves repeatedly, we can remember them by starting to recite the initial words or parts of that concept. You can also connect your subject matter with things that you already know to facilitate better learning. This is also known as elaborative encoding, wherein your brain connects new information through old data that it already has.

As such, while dual encoding definitely has its advantages, you must also utilize the two other types of encoding for maximum learning, regardless of which topic you're studying.

Takeaways

- There are various science-based tips we can implement into our learning routines to maximize the information we retain from our study sessions. These include things like self-explanation, wherein we use our existing knowledge to acquire new information through the use of analogies and comparisons. This is a method of self-testing that allows you to identify blind spots rather quickly.

- Another incredibly useful trick is to introduce variety into our learning methods. Whether this be shifting our physical locations while learning or reading about different topics simultaneously, variety helps our brain absorb information into our long-term memory much more effectively than when we stick to one topic and study it in one physical location throughout. This is because information is often context-specific.
- Besides the things we do while learning, we must also focus on the things we do while we aren't studying. Elements like sleep and exercise have time and again been proven to enhance how much information we can retain, and we must focus on those activities to ensure we remain as productive as possible. While sleep is when our brain consolidates new information that we received while awake, exercise makes us alert and more receptive to learning, especially if we exercise just before studying.

Unfortunately, both of these factors are often overlooked or shirked in favor of blindly trying to learn more and more.

- Two more techniques that have proven valuable in helping us learn better are self-testing, and the use of dual coding. Study after study has shown that students who take tests on new information consistently perform better than those who don't. Though testing is usually considered a stressful affair, it is truly beneficial, one that we must learn to become comfortable with. This is more commonly known as retrieval practice, and it's the exercise of pulling information out of your brain.

- On the other hand, dual coding involves representing new information using both visual and text-based cues. Though some topics are tricky to portray using visual aids, we can make use of different tools such as mind maps, flow charts, etc., alongside simple written text.

The aim is to give information more methods of sticking in your long-term memory.

Summary Guide

Chapter One. Your Obstacles Are Everyone's Obstacles

- Learning new things to increase your knowledge and skill set sounds good in theory, but many of us hesitate to try learning something new. We cite common excuses like not having enough time, not having access to good resources, or fearing failure in new endeavors. Our years in school have left us with the impression that learning is one-dimensional and utterly boring. Yet this is far from the case. Here is where learning *how* to learn becomes so important.
- Those of us who are afraid to learn are often unknowingly suffering from a fixed mindset. This way of thinking assumes that people are born with a static set of qualities and talents that never change. If we aren't immediately successful at something,

we just don't have what it takes. Yet this sort of thinking is extraordinarily unhelpful, as it prevents us from exposing ourselves to new skills and knowledge. Fixed mindsets are particularly common in people who fear failure, have low self-esteem, or excuse themselves by pretending to be too busy. For them, failure isn't a natural part of learning, but a damning indictment of one's abilities. They fail to recognize that mistakes are as natural as breathing, and that learning well necessarily involves failing, and failing repeatedly.

- However, if we adopt a growth mindset wherein the possibilities for development and expansion are endless, we find that we are much more open to learning, as well as failure in learning. Some common issues that people face when trying to learn new things include not forming their goals properly, and failing to discover good resources to study. While both of these issues are surmountable for those with a growth mindset, they become impossible to overcome if you have a fixed mindset that refuses to consider more than one option. As such, cultivating a growth mindset is essential to learning new skills and acquiring more knowledge.

Chapter Two. The Double Loop Framework

- There are two main models of learning: single and double loop learning. Single loop learning is the way we have been taught to acquire new information all throughout our schooling years. This is the method that simply involves performing certain actions (for example, rote learning) to achieve certain outcomes (doing well in examinations). Here, the emphasis isn't on the learning itself, but the purpose for which we are learning.
- One major drawback of single loop learning is the way it handles errors and mistakes. If you make one, there isn't really a good way to resolve that

besides simply doing something different (say, rote learning more effectively). We never consider the underlying causes of our errors, instead dealing with them only on a superficial level.
- This is where double loop learning shines. It's a method of information synthesis and processing. Though harder and more involved than single loop learning, it is substantially more effective at facilitating learning. Here, we constantly utilize feedback and our own introspection to evolve the ways in which we learn. We repeatedly question the methods and steps we follow, as well as why we're following them in the first place. Instead of simply scoring well in examinations, we learn for the sake of learning, which in turn helps us generate curiosity for our subject matter. This results in holistic learning, which helps us achieve our initial goal of scoring well too.
- Those with a fixed mindset are generally more likely to learn

through single loop mechanisms due to the comfort and lack of self-reflection involved. On the other hand, those with a growth mindset are more naturally attuned to double loop learning. It is often hard to look at ourselves and accept that we may be the ones who have a fixed mindset or follow single loop learning mechanisms, but the first step to being able to learn better is to recognize the mistakes we are making in the present. This inevitably involves getting comfortable with failure, since that is unavoidable.

Chapter Three. Reading 2.0

- Reading is undoubtedly the best way to gather new information on any given topic. Each subject has tons of written material dedicated to it; we just need to find the resources that most closely sync with our motivations behind studying a particular topic. Yet, even if we discover these resources, how do we read in a way that helps us retain the most information? How can we maximize our learning through the written word? The first step here is to just take some time out to read from our busy schedules.

- Mortimer Adler has outlined four distinct steps that describe how exactly we should read in order to derive the most benefit from it. If you're reading this, you've already completed the first step, which is learning how to read. Following that, you need to learn how to identify resources worth reading. This can be done by skimming through parts of a book and seeing whether it appeals to our interests. Once we find some suitable books, we utilize analytical reading, wherein you closely analyze what it is that you're reading. Figure out the main thesis of your book, what genre or category it falls under, the historical context of the author's arguments, etc. Lastly, read several different books on the same subject

and compare the arguments they present in what is known as syntopical reading.
- When it comes to selecting the best reading material, follow the PROMPT technique. This stands for Presentation, Relevance, Objectivity, Method, Provenance, and Timeliness. Consider all of these factors and evaluate resources based on them. Each refers to an aspect of different resources that make them worth considering.
- Finally, the SQ3R method for extracting information from a resource. Use it. It stands for survey, question, read, recite, review. This is not just a process for attacking a book, but rather a plan for tackling entire disciplines and fields—and whatever you are trying to learn for yourself. Most people will use some elements of the SQ3R method, such as the read and review portion, but without the other elements, deeper comprehension is rarer and more difficult.

Chapter Four. Just Ask

- As children, we once asked hundreds of questions a day to satisfy our natural curiosities. However, as adults, we increasingly refrain from expressing our doubts out of fear of appearing stupid or from a tame acceptance of things as the way they are. However, asking probing and relevant questions is the best way to aggregate answers that challenge our preconceived notions and foster expansions of knowledge. The best questions expose our ignorance and assumptions about the world that didn't have any concrete basis, forcing us to think in new and better ways.
- To ask better questions, we must be aware of the different types of questions that exist. We have elicitation questions, which are used to answer "how," "why," "what," "where," etc. We also have divergent questions, open-ended queries that

don't have a specifically right answer. Next, we can utilize elaboration questions to seek more information about something by asking "what else...?" type doubts. Clarification questions, as the name suggests, aim to resolve any potential misunderstandings or wrongly held assumptions. Heuristic questions focus on the method of questioning that we are utilizing over their content. Lastly, inventive questions are radically creative questions that can be used to juxtapose one piece or information with another through analogies or comparisons. This helps us understand complex concepts through the knowledge we already possess.

- Ask questions about anything and everything related to your subject matter. From the author's intentions, to the idiosyncrasies of his or her writing style, the motivations behind making certain arguments, the methodologies the author uses, and

everything in between, all of it is worth putting under the scanner.
- Another helpful framework for questions comes from Socrates. He put forth a set of six types of questions for critical thinking, deeper understanding, and peeling back the layers of just about anything. These types of questions include: clarifying, probing assumptions, probing reasoning and analysis, probing viewpoints and perspectives, probing implications, and probing the question or assertion itself.
- If we fail to answer our questions ourselves, there is no shame in seeking help. Make use of online forums that are dedicated to the topic you're trying to study. They likely exist—you just need to find them.

Chapter Five. Notes as Your Second Brain

- Being able to read large amounts of text is of no use if we don't have an effective way to remember the information we come across. Our memories are not capable of retaining everything we read, and so we need an efficient system of note-taking to aid us in remembering as much information as we can.
- Not only does note-taking help us remember more by writing important concepts or ideas in concise and easy language, we inevitably engage with our content in creative ways when we assemble information in a systematic manner.
- The sociologist Niklas Luhmann devised a system of note-taking that is still held in high regard decades after its genesis. Besides his elaborate system itself, there is much to learn from the way Luhmann treated note-taking. This includes treating note-taking as a process that

facilitates new and creative ideas instead of simply being a repository of those we have already thought of. Taking notes demands a standardized workflow that must be followed to maximize productivity. We must also treat our notes as if they are going to be presented to an audience. This encourages us to compile them in a manner that is aesthetically and logically appealing enough to be revisited for future reference. The more notes we make, the better. As long as we have an efficient way to sort them, they are bound to be helpful to our purpose of learning. As we make more and more notes, we must also regularly appraise our progress and rectify any errors that might have previously escaped our notice.

- Other useful tips for making effective notes include using abbreviations and shorthand to minimize the amount of space taken by words and denotations. Using different colors to highlight or mark unique sub-topics also aids us in accessing specific concepts within vast, complex subjects. Having said that, keep things as simple as you can. You don't need an elaborate note-taking system if a minimal one does the trick.

Chapter Six. Lessons from the Science of Learning

- There are various science-based tips we can implement into our learning routines to maximize the information we retain from our study sessions. These include things like self-explanation, wherein we use our existing knowledge to acquire new information through the use of analogies and comparisons. This is a method of self-testing that allows you to identify blind spots rather quickly.

- Another incredibly useful trick is to introduce variety into our learning methods. Whether this be shifting our physical locations while learning or reading about different topics simultaneously, variety helps our

brain absorb information into our long-term memory much more effectively than when we stick to one topic and study it in one physical location throughout. This is because information is often context-specific.
- Besides the things we do while learning, we must also focus on the things we do while we aren't studying. Elements like sleep and exercise have time and again been proven to enhance how much information we can retain, and we must focus on those activities to ensure we remain as productive as possible. While sleep is when our brain consolidates new information that we received while awake, exercise makes us alert and more receptive to learning, especially if we exercise just before studying. Unfortunately, both of these factors are often overlooked or shirked in favor of blindly trying to learn more and more.
- Two more techniques that have proven valuable in helping us learn

better are self-testing, and the use of dual coding. Study after study has shown that students who take tests on new information consistently perform better than those who don't. Though testing is usually considered a stressful affair, it is truly beneficial, one that we must learn to become comfortable with. This is more commonly known as retrieval practice, and it's the exercise of pulling information out of your brain.

- On the other hand, dual coding involves representing new information using both visual and text-based cues. Though some topics are tricky to portray using visual aids, we can make use of different tools such as mind maps, flow charts, etc., alongside simple written text. The aim is to give information more methods of sticking in your long-term memory.

Printed by Amazon Italia Logistica S.r.l.
Torrazza Piemonte (TO), Italy